Great Rooms!
How to Organize Your Classroom for Effective Learning

Grades K–1

By

Barbara Allman

Published by Frank Schaffer Publications
an imprint of

 **Children's Publishing**

Author: Barbara Allman
Editor: Sara Freeman

Children's Publishing

Published by Frank Schaffer Publications
An imprint of McGraw-Hill Children's Publishing
Copyright © 2004 McGraw-Hill Children's Publishing

Send all inquiries to:
McGraw-Hill Children's Publishing
3195 Wilson Drive NW
Grand Rapids, Michigan 49544

Great Rooms! How to Organize Your Classroom for Effective Learning—grades K–1
ISBN: 0-7682-2607-4

1 2 3 4 5 6 7 8 9 MAL 09 08 07 06 05 04

Table of Contents

0-7682-2607-4 *Great Rooms! Grades K–1*

Introduction

Great Rooms! How to Organize Your Classroom for Effective Learning gives you valuable insights and practical tips that will save you time and effort as you work towards producing a stimulating learning environment. When you are prepared and organized, the everyday tasks of teaching become easier, classroom management is achieved with confidence, and you are left with more time and energy to do what you love to do best—teach children.

This book includes information that pertains to classroom setup and seating arrangements, sections on effective discipline techniques, and important strategies for positive communications. Creative ideas abound for instilling a bright and welcoming classroom with eye-catching displays that engage and interest learners. There are useful lists for substitute teacher preparation, special events and field trips, learning center projects and preparations, and volunteers in the classroom.

Establishing a warm and open environment starts even before your students enter the classroom for the first time. Setting up your classroom for maximum learning builds a sense of safety where students will feel that they are free to learn, experiment, and grow as life-long learners.

You will find that you will have more time for one-on-one conferences, small group remediation or whole class enrichment, once the tools are set in place to maximize "up" time for effective learning. The routines, interactive decoratives, schedules, forms and letters are effective vehicles for communication, which is the first step in building a sense of community beyond the physical environment of the classroom.

Positive reinforcement ideas, self-esteem incentives, awards, engaging learning centers, realistic grade expectations, and a sense of order, set the stage for a smooth and productive learning environment.

If working smarter—not harder—is your goal, the strategies in *Great Rooms! How to Organize Your Classroom for Effective Learning* will become your essential resource for creating a vibrant and effective environment with a strong sense of community built on trust, fairness and the necessary skills invaluable for effective learning.

Show and Tell time is fun!

Chapter 1: Classroom Environment

Read this chapter to find out about:

- room arrangements to facilitate learning
- eye-catching bulletin boards and displays
- using the whiteboard to the best advantage
- organizing and maintaining supplies
- storage solutions
- building and organizing a classroom library
- miscellaneous ideas for an efficient classroom

A Place of Their Own

Room arrangements for kindergarten and first grade classrooms are dependent upon the type of furniture supplied by the school. Individual student desks are sometimes an option, but tables that seat two or more are common in the early grades. If your students have their own desks, they will be able to store their supplies at hand. If classroom tables do not have storage spaces under them, and even if they do, consider providing separate cubbyholes for each child to store folders, pencils, papers, and other necessities.

Label each student's desk or table space with their name. Commercial nametags are available, but a simple sentence strip cut to size works well, too. A nametag printed clearly in manuscript will serve several purposes. It labels the child's space or desk, it helps the child learn to identify their name, and it also serves as a handwriting model. Laminating the nametags makes them more durable. Secure the nametags to the desktop with tape or clear contact paper. It is a good idea to check with the school office as to what types of adhesives are recommended.

Cubbyholes

Student cubbyholes have the advantage of being away from the workspace where children will be focusing on the task at hand. This means fewer distractions during work time. It also encourages children to organize for work and to think ahead about what supplies they will need to take to their desk or worktable. Be sure to label the cubbyholes with the children's names or, if you like, label each with a photo of the child.

Rug Area

An area rug in your classroom can serve as a focal point for activities. A large area rug provides a space where all the children can sit for story time and circle time activities. Small mats also provide individual spaces for children to sit. You may be able to obtain carpet samples from a local carpet store for this purpose. Individual mats encourage children to have their own personal space and not crowd others. The mats can be neatly stacked when not in use.

Classroom Environment

Room Arrangement

Choose a room arrangement that accommodates your teaching style and the children's needs. Some teachers wish to start the year with a simple, standard arrangement of tables or desks in rows, with the teacher's desk to one side at the front. This allows the teacher to get to know the class and observe children's work habits. As routines are established, reading groups are formed, and centers are introduced, the room arrangement can be modified.

Basic Arrangement

- Desks or tables facing chalkboard at front
- Teacher's desk at front
- Reading table at front
- Circle time area at back
- Cubbyholes at back

Long Tables Arrangement

- Tables linked in rows facing chalkboard
- Bookcase divides tables from circle area in back
- Reading table at back, teacher facing children
- Teacher's desk at back

Group Work Arrangement

- Tables or desks in groups seating four children
- Seats angled toward chalkboard for easy sight lines
- Reading table and circle time area to one side

Classroom Environment

A Peaceful Place

Children sometimes need a quiet place in the busy classroom where they can go for comfort, relaxation, or self-control. Allow one or two children at a time in the peaceful place. Design your quiet corner with any of the following:

- pillows
- a green houseplant
- classical music tapes
- a bean bag chair
- a travel poster of a peaceful place
- a stuffed animal

Computer Corner

After your students have received instruction on how to operate the classroom computer, they may be able to complete simple tasks independently. If possible, place the computer near a bulletin board or chalkboard where instructions and rules for its use can be posted, either printed or in picture form. Store printing paper at the computer table or nearby for easy access.

Sight Lines

When arranging the classroom, keep in mind that children need to be able to see the teacher clearly and easily without straining or turning around. Some students may have learning disabilities or vision problems that are exacerbated by having to look to the side instead of straight ahead. These problems may not even have been identified in young children. Be alert to this when planning your seating arrangement.

Classroom Environment

Welcome New Students

It is a good idea to have an extra desk and chair on hand in the classroom for a new student. Tuck inside the desk a welcome card, new work folder, pencil, and other basics. Especially if your school is in an area where new homes are being built or where the population fluctuates with the seasons, it is very likely you will have new arrivals with no advance notice. Showing the new student to their very own desk is a nice way to give them an immediate warm welcome.

Study Carrels

Individual tabletop study carrels are useful in the primary classroom. They can help students focus their attention on a task by blocking out distractions. Make study carrels from sturdy cardboard folded into three panels so they stand independently. Commercial display boards can also be cut down to form carrels. Trim down the side panels if you wish. Use colorful duct tape to finish all the edges. Large clips can hold a paper with instructions or work to be copied by the student. A daily schedule or check-off list may also be attached to the carrel in this way. Use giant rubber bands to hold supplies. On the back of the carrel, post a reminder such as "Do Not Disturb: Child at Work."

Work Areas

There are many ways to create work spaces in the classroom. Consider using the following as dividers or space definers:

- bookcases
- small rugs
- easels and chart stands
- a low platform
- a curtain on a spring rod
- bulletin board or wall display

0-7682-2607-4 *Great Rooms! Grades K–1*

Eye-Catching Bulletin Boards and Displays

Welcome to Our Class

Create a display to welcome your students on the first day of school. A friendly welcome sign at the children's eye level on the inside of the door helps establish a warm atmosphere. It will also help parents identify your classroom. Decorate it with a favorite cartoon character or cuddly animal and label it with your name and grade. A sign on the back of the door or on the wall next to the door will help identify your class when the door is closed as well.

Spreading Sunshine

The back of a bookcase placed near the door is the perfect spot for a welcome display. Take a photo of each child on the first day, and post them on a large yellow sun cut from poster board and taped to the bookcase. Write "Classroom Sunbeams" on a sentence strip to headline the display. Use removable tape so the photos can be reused throughout the year in displays and activities.

Busy Bee Classroom Helpers

A *Classroom Helpers* display is a useful bulletin board in the primary classroom. A helpers bulletin board should have interchangeable parts to allow you to change helpers regularly so that each child has an opportunity to do each job. Use the bee pattern on page 12 to create your own friendly display. Make a copy for each child. Have the children write their names on the bees, color, and cut them out along with the separate wing pieces. Post the bees on a bulletin board around a yellow construction paper hive. Write a classroom job on each separate wing. Laminating the bees and wings will make them more durable. To assign jobs, tack the wings on the bees. You will probably have more wings than jobs, so you can write "buzz" on the extras. Here are some classroom jobs to consider:

- Messengers
- Paper passers
- Mail delivery
- Board cleaners
- Room inspector
- Supply organizer

- Playground equipment manager
- Window checker
- Pet care
- Plant care
- Line leader

0-7682-2607-4 *Great Rooms! Grades K–1*

Eye-Catching Bulletin Boards and Displays

Happy Birthday Cupcake

A birthday display in the primary classroom acknowledges that everyone has a day to feel special. Make copies of the pattern on page 14. Have each child write their name on a birthday cupcake, color it, and cut it out. You may want to have an aide, parent volunteer, or upper-grade helper pre-cut the designs for kindergarten students. Write the date of each child's birthday on the candle flame of their cupcake. Title a bulletin board "Happy Birthday to You!" Make a sentence strip with the name of each month. Arrange the cupcakes by month above the corresponding sentence strips, as if on plates.

To celebrate each child's birthday, write a birthday message on chart paper, read it together, have each class member sign it, and give it to the birthday child as a keepsake.

Today is October 12, 2004. It is Violet's birthday. She is five years old. Happy Birthday, Violet!

> *Love from your class,*

> (Signatures of students and teacher)

Poet-Tree Place

A poetry display helps to enrich the literacy environment of the classroom. Even pre-readers can learn to recite a choral poem. Make a bulletin board display with the outline of a large tree with leaves that can be changed with the seasons. The children can help by creating the leaves. Make a space beside the tree for a sheet of chart paper. Print an appropriate poem on chart paper and post it beside the Poet-Tree. Visit the poem each day, recite it together, track the words, and have the children point to the words they know. Be sure to give each child a copy of the poem when it comes down and is replaced by a new one. (See page 15.)

Happy Birthday Cupcake Pattern

0-7682-2607-4 *Great Rooms! Grades K-1*

Name_____ Date_____

A Poem I Have Learned

0-7682-2607-4 *Great Rooms! Grades K–1*

Eye-Catching Bulletin Boards and Displays

Participatory Bulletin Boards

Involve your students in making bulletin boards on which to display their best work. The children can make a collage, covering all or part of the bulletin board, then post their best papers on it. For example, when studying the rain forest, have the children create a colorful and exotic rain forest environment thick with trees and rain forest inhabitants. Save all construction paper scraps in a scrap box for this purpose. Assign different groups to draw and cut out flora and fauna of the forest. Staple their creations to cover one entire area of the bulletin board. The same technique might be used when studying the community, the zoo, the ocean, and other topics.

Paper Chains for Bulletin Boards

Cut strips of colored paper and have the children create paper chains to decorate a bulletin board. Orange chains can be stapled to the bulletin board to form a giant pumpkin for fall. White chains can form a snowman for winter, and yellow and green paper chains can be used to create a huge spring flower. Paper chains can also be used to create borders for the bulletin board. Post the children's favorite artwork celebrating the season.

Bulletin Board Photo Album

What was on last year's bulletin board about seeds and plants? A good way to keep track of your successful bulletin boards is with a photo album. Take the time to photograph a completed bulletin board. Keep a disposable camera on hand labeled for this purpose. When the photos are developed at the end of the year, you will have time to organize them into an album. You might also number the photos and then label the bulletin board pieces with the same number before storing them. In this way, it will be a quick and easy task to assemble the board the next time.

Eye-Catching Bulletin Boards and Displays

Bulletin Board Tips

Here are some ideas to save you time and effort in planning and creating bulletin boards for your classroom.

- Have on hand a kit with tools you will need to assemble the board—stapler, extra staples, scissors, trim, photo reference, letters, pencil, and pins. Having these supplies on hand will save walking across the room to retrieve each one. Use a cleaning supplies tote or a carpenter's apron for your kit.

- Plan your bulletin boards so the same background color can be used all year, or at least for several different displays. For example, a yellow background will work for September's scarecrow, October's pumpkin, and November's Thanksgiving turkey. Blue might be used for the winter months and green for spring and summer.

- Save time during the year by layering background colors. Put up several colors at a time and simply remove the top layer when you want to change colors. Your new background color is already in place.

- Before you head for the office or workroom to get bulletin board paper, be sure to measure and note the dimensions of your bulletin board to take with you, and file for future reference.

- Store lettering for each bulletin board in a separate envelope labeled with the display title. Paper clip the letters together to spell out the words in the order in which they appear in the title.

- Gather the materials needed and hand over a diagram or photo of the bulletin board to a parent volunteer to assemble the bulletin board for you. Keep diagrams in a notebook for future use.

- Use fabric, a colorful plastic picnic tablecloth, or wrapping paper to make an interesting bulletin board background.

Tabletop Displays

Use fold-up cardboard display boards to create learning centers. Spruce up the display boards by applying decorative borders and letters to them. Directions and illustrations can be clipped to the board with binder clips for easy removal and replacement.

Eye-Catching Bulletin Boards and Displays

Classroom Signs

Signs posted around the classroom can help establish a print-rich environment for beginning readers. The signs placed around the room should have meaning for the children and demonstrate that writing has a purpose. For example, write a numbered list of simple directions telling how to accomplish a specific task at a station or center. Chances are the children will remember the directions better if you write them with the children. This introduction will help them learn the directions independently.

Doorknob Signs

Place a doorknob sign on your door to indicate to visitors or school personnel where your class is when you leave the room. Examples: *We are at recess. We are at Music. We are in the gym.* Pages 19–20 have four doorknob signs that you can color, cut out, and laminate for durability. Invite the Line Leader to read aloud the sign and place it on the doorknob.

More Signs

Here are other signs with a purpose for the classroom:

- Listening center directions
- Directions for computer use
- Labels on drawers and other storage spaces indicating their contents
- Schedule for the day
- Lists of group members
- Signs in the library corner advertising good books
- Signs stating where things belong: *Hang your jacket here. Lunch boxes go here.*

Eye-Catching Bulletin Boards and Displays

Teacher's Bulletin Board

Set aside a small bulletin board, an area of a larger bulletin board, or hang your own small corkboard strictly for teacher's use. Post schedules, notes, reminders, and office memos that you must refer to. This will help ensure that these papers do not get shuffled or lost under other paperwork.

Display Your Credentials

Hang your diploma, teaching certificate or license, and professional awards in nice frames in a prominent spot on a wall, just as members of other professions do. If there is room, you may want to set aside a small shelf, tabletop, or additional bulletin board of pictures of your family and pets, and images of your favorite activities or hobbies. This is a great way to initiate a positive and friendly relationship with your students.

Doorknob Signs

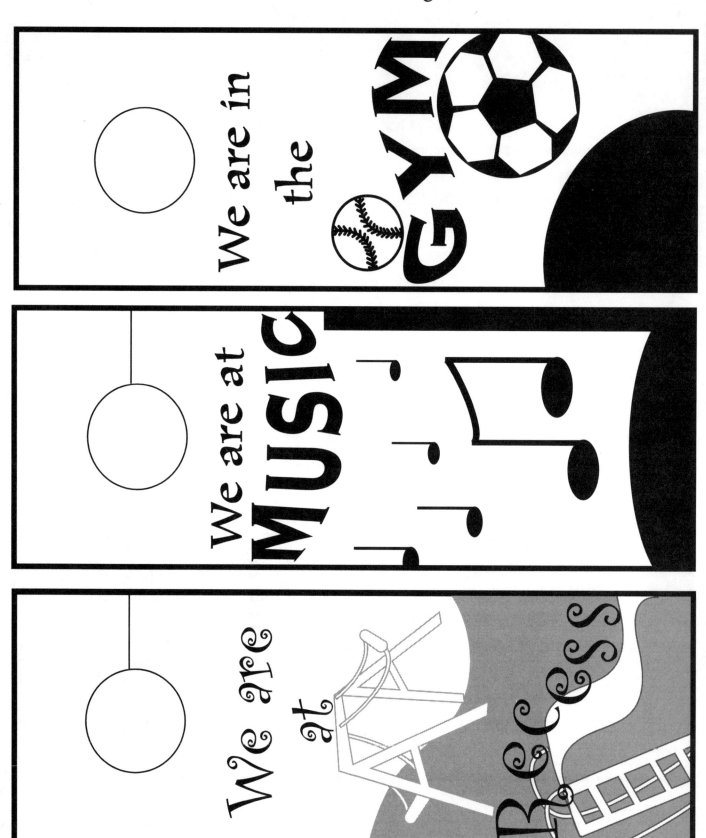

0-7682-2607-4 *Great Rooms!* *Grades K–1*

Eye-Catching Bulletin Boards and Displays

Alphabet Border

An alphabet border is an essential tool in the early grade classroom. It helps remind students how to form the letters. If it is a picture border, it also reminds them of the letter sounds. Commercial borders are available—but a very effective alphabet can be made with 26 pieces of 8 1/2" x 11" poster board. On each card, print an uppercase and lowercase letter using the handwriting style adopted in your school. Then illustrate each one with a coloring book picture. Distribute the pictures and have the children color, cut out, and glue them to the alphabet cards. Laminate the cards for durability and hang them on the wall where they can be easily seen.

Numbers and Number Words

A number chart or border is another basic for the kindergarten or first grade classroom. It's easy to create your own chart or border that will add to the children's fun as they learn number concepts. Using colorful poster board, make a separate card for each number. Or use one larger piece for a 1–10 chart if you wish. Print the number and use miniature party favors or decorations to illustrate it. Glue the favors to the chart with a glue gun. (Children should not be allowed to use a hot glue gun.) Example: one miniature book, two noisemakers, three miniature dolls, four toy trucks, five paper umbrellas, six rings, seven finger puppets, eight lollipops, nine stickers, ten seashells.

Beginning Word Walls

Introduce word walls to your students by using their names. Make columns on sheets of chart paper, labeling each with a letter of the alphabet. Hang them at the children's eye level. Give each child an index card with his name printed on it. Have children glue their card under the letter that starts their name. Use the charts for word wall activities, such as reading all the names that begin with C, pointing to one's own name, counting the names that begin with L, and so on.

0-7682-2607-4 *Great Rooms! Grades K–1*

Using the Whiteboard to the Best Advantage

Whiteboard Activities for Motor Skills

Young children may need to develop gross motor skills before they are able to master small motor skills required in writing and reading. Create activities that will help your students gain control over large muscle movement. Set up an overhead projector near a whiteboard or chalkboard. Make transparencies of large coloring book pictures. Look for pictures that have a variety of lines—straight, curving, zigzag, spiraling, and circular. Place a transparency on the overhead and show the children how to trace the giant picture projected onto the board. Have them shut off the projector to see their finished picture, then erase the picture to prepare for the next child to have a turn. You can also create transparencies of large letters and numbers for children to trace.

Individual Wipe-Off Boards

Make individual wipe-off boards from sturdy cardboard covered with black adhesive-backed paper. Children can write on the boards with chalk for individual response activities and use a sock to erase their work. The same boards can be made using white adhesive-backed paper. Using water soluble markers and a moist paper towel makes these boards erasable. Children can use these during group work to write their answers and hold them up for you to see.

Whiteboard Reward

Most children love to write and draw on the board. Use this as an incentive or reward. For example, the students with the most good behavior points or who finish all their math pages can be given ten minutes of free time at the board at the end of the week. Students who score 100 on their spelling test can practice next week's words at the board instead of on paper.

Using the Whiteboard to the Best Advantage

Special Spaces on the Board

Establish an area of the whiteboard in your classroom where children will know to look regularly for information. Be consistent about where you write these items. Here are some items you may want to include:

- **Today's Special Events**—Write a brief message to the class about what they will be doing in school today. *Dear Class, Today we will make our Mother's Day gifts.*

- **Our Daily News**—As an end-of-the-day activity, have the children dictate what the class did today. Write two or three items under today's date. Assign a child to write this in a class journal the following day.

- **Word of the Day**—Select a word that the children need or want to know. Read it together, discuss it, and have several children use it in a sentence. Choose one of the sentences and write it on the board. Have the children write the word, write the sentence, and illustrate the sentence. Before going home, give the children an index card with the word of the day on it. Have them bring it back the next day and read it to you as their ticket to enter the classroom. They can file their words in a file box with alphabet dividers. Their word box can be used whenever they need words for writing activities.

- **Question of the Day**—This is a question the children can answer from their own personal experience. Writing the question and their answer might be the first thing they do in the morning. Examples: *What would you name a pet cat? Have you ever eaten a tortilla? What is your favorite color?*

- **Homework**—Write reminders of homework assignments, items to take home or to bring in from home, and so on.

- **Poem of the Week**—Write a short poem that the children can learn to recite together during transitional times.

- **Motto for the Week**—Write a short motto or positive statement for children to copy at the top of each paper they write, after their name.

Using the Whiteboard to the Best Advantage

Games to Play at the Board

Most children enjoy having a turn to write on and erase the board. Use the whiteboard to play motivating games, to reinforce basic skills.

What's My Consonant Sound?—Divide the class into two teams. Have one child from each team stand at the board. Say a word that begins with a consonant. The first child to write the consonant wins a point for her team. Play another version by having the children listen for and write the ending consonant. To keep the entire class involved, have teammates write the answers in the air until it is their turn at the board.

Look for the Blend—Write several words that begin with different blends on the board. Call on a child to come to the board. Say one of the words. The child finds the word, reads it aloud, and erases it. Continue until all the words are erased.

Climb the Ladder—Review color words, number words, or other sight words with this activity. Draw a ladder on the board. On each rung, write a color word. Ask one child at a time to climb the ladder by reading the words, starting at the bottom.

Which Spelling Word Is Missing?—Write all the week's spelling words on the board and read them aloud together. Have the children put their heads down on their desks and cover their eyes while you erase a word from the board. Have them look at the board again and try to name the missing word. Call on a child to say and spell the word.

Word Wall Words—If you have a word wall in your classroom, play this game to review some of the words. Draw boxes on the board that show the configuration of a word from the word wall. As a further clue, write the first letter of the word in the corresponding box. Have a child come to the board and write in the remainder of the word.

0-7682-2607-4 *Great Rooms! Grades K–1*

Using the Whiteboard to the Best Advantage

WELCOME

Whiteboard Stories

Use the whiteboard creatively and effectively for storytelling activities. Storytelling can boost your students' language and listening skills. Pages 26–29 feature stories you can tell while you make a simple line drawing on the board. Each story reveals a surprise picture at the end.

Presenting Stories at the Whiteboard

Don't worry if you can't draw! The stories on pages 26–29 are told using simple step-by-step line drawings. Here are some helpful hints:

- Read over the story and practice it before presenting it to the class.

- Draw the picture on the whiteboard as you tell the story.

- Face the children as much as possible as you tell the story.

- Hold the story script in your hand as you present it, or memorize it if you like.

- When you come to a blank line in the story, have the children tell you the missing word.

Follow-Up for Whiteboard Stories

Involve your students in an enjoyable learning activity to follow up the whiteboard stories. It will help you evaluate your students' recall. After presenting a story, draw the picture again step by step. Give the children a copy of the activity sheet on page 30 and show them how to copy your drawing. Next, instruct the children to write their version of the story on a piece of writing paper. Attach each child's story to their picture and hang the papers on a bulletin board.

Expanding the Whiteboard Stories

Your students will enjoy hearing the whiteboard stories again and again. As they become familiar with each story, you may wish to write a continuation of it. Encourage the children to help you add new events to the story and other characters or objects to the drawing.

Whiteboard Story—Barnyard Surprise

Early one morning a strange white ball appeared in the middle of the barnyard.

After a while, it made a little scratching noise.

Soon a pig jogged over to see it. He tried to figure out what it was, but he couldn't.

Then there was another little scratching noise.

The barnyard cat sneaked over to see it. She tried to figure out what it was too, but she couldn't.

As the cat and pig were staring at the ball, they spotted a tiny hole in it.

All at once there were two quick pecks. To their surprise, the ball cracked open and out popped a ____.

Of course, it was a baby chick! The white thing was really an ____.

Yes, it was an egg!

0-7682-2607-4 *Great Rooms! Grades K–1*

Whiteboard Story—The Magic Kitchen

This is a magic kitchen.

In this kitchen there was a lovely teapot.

She had a beautiful handle . . .

. . . and a gently curving spout.

Even though she was loved and well cared for, she yearned more than anything else to see the outside world. Every night she dreamed of a place with a shining lake . . .

. . . swaying palm trees . . .

. . . and smooth rocks.

One miraculous morning, she opened her eyes. She looked at herself and realized that she was no longer a teapot. She had turned into an _____. That's right, an elephant!

She smiled a big smile.

Then she waved good-bye to her happy home and bounded across the land to see what she could see.

Whiteboard Story—Andrew's Hill

Near Andrew's house was a hill where he liked to go. It was his own special place.

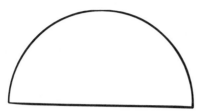

One day Andrew climbed up his hill . . .

. . . perched on a big rock and looked out.

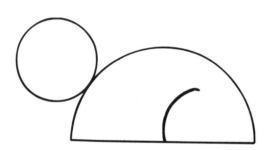

In the distance he spotted two mountains, . . .

. . . a couple of ponds, and . . .

. . . four little roads.

When he gazed up into the sky, he saw a big robin soar by.

Suddenly, he heard a rustle in a nearby bush. Andrew discovered that he was sharing his hill with someone else. Who was it? _____ Yes, it was a friendly cat!

0-7682-2607-4 *Great Rooms! Grades K–1*

Whiteboard Story—The Traveling Triangle

Once upon a time there was a little triangle.

He wanted to go to the moon.

He asked his friend Rectangle how to get there.

Rectangle said, "Go north." So the little triangle did. But all he saw was snow.

So he talked to his friends the Triangle Twins.

They replied, "Go south." So the little triangle followed their advice. But all he found were clouds.

Feeling discouraged, the little triangle went back home and sat by the window. What do you think he spotted? _____ Yes, it was a rocket ship!

So he climbed aboard and flew to the moon.

0-7682-2607-4 *Great Rooms! Grades K–1*

Name_____ Date_____

My Sketch

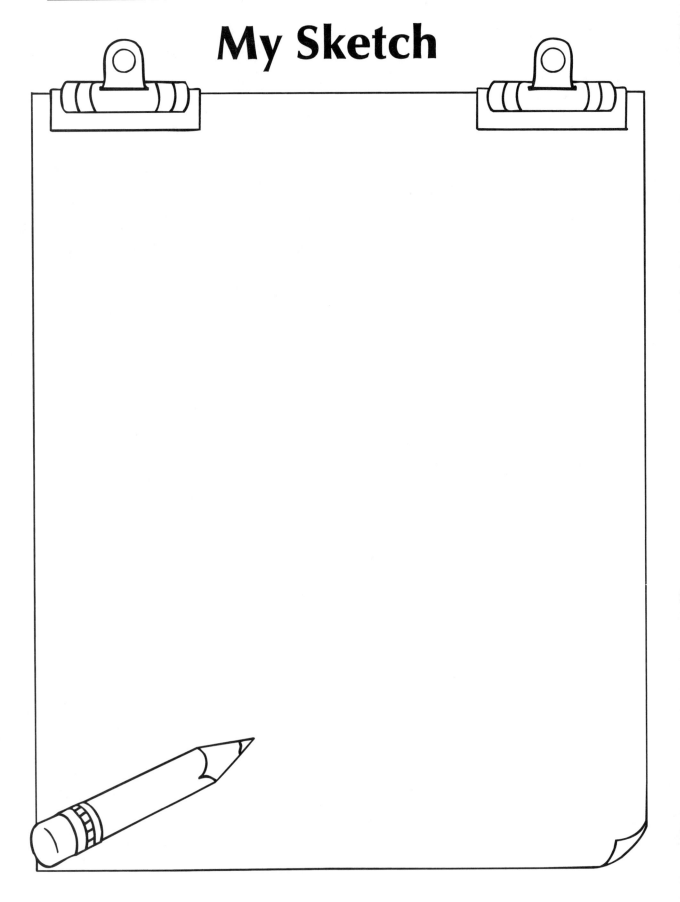

0-7682-2607-4 *Great Rooms! Grades K–1*

Organizing and Maintaining Supplies

Pencil Supply

Setting up some pencil guidelines and organization can save valuable instructional time in the classroom.

- You may find that the pencil allotment the school provides needs to be supplemented. If you have children bring in their own pencils, request that parents only send yellow No. 2 pencils. This will avoid tears over specially colored or cartoon character pencils that get lost.

- One method to store pencils is to provide a pencil can for each group of student tables. Cover a juice can with colorful adhesive-backed paper for this purpose. Be sure cans have no sharp edges.

- To keep the pencil cans from spilling, place a Velcro® strip on the bottom of each can and on a plastic place mat on each table.

- Teach the children to store their pencils in the can unless they need sharpening.

- Place a tray or basket labeled *Please Sharpen* on the supply table or near the pencil sharpener. Place a pencil can with sharpened pencils near it. Teach the children to place their broken pencils or pencils in need of sharpening in the tray. Then, they can take a new pencil from the can. Appoint a helper each week to be the pencil-sharpening assistant. The assistant sharpens the pencils in the tray once a day. The helper places them in the can. No one else is allowed to sharpen pencils.

Catalog Orders

Save the teacher's supply catalogs you receive in a magazine storage box. This will allow you to browse through them readily when you are in need of materials, resources, furniture, or storage solutions. You can simply copy a page to request the school office order a specific item. You can also easily research materials while you are lesson planning.

Tissue Supply

By encouraging your students to use a tissue when they have the sniffles, you will find that your classroom uses a large supply of tissues. Request that each child bring in a box of tissues at the beginning of the year. Place a box or two in prominent places where children will always know to look for them, such as near the sink or on a bookcase. Store the remainder of the boxes in a cupboard or closet until they are needed.

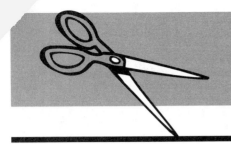

More On Supplies

Student Supplies

The key to maintaining student supplies is "a place for everything and everything in its place." Provide plastic baskets at each student table for crayons and markers. Store student scissors in a plastic basket turned upside down. Make sure it is deep enough so that scissors can be suspended points down inside the holes in the bottom of the basket. Or, turn an egg carton upside down and poke a hole in each bump so scissors can be inserted for storage.

Paper Scraps

Cleanup is easy when children know that all colored construction paper scraps go in the scrap box. Use a cardboard carton covered with colorful adhesive-backed paper for this. Place a label on it. The scrap box makes it easy for children to access scraps for many creative projects throughout the year.

Supply Organizers

Provide easy access to often-used supplies by placing them in labeled containers. Less-often used supplies can be stored in cupboards or closets and should also be labeled. The following containers are useful for organizing and storing supplies. Using uniform sizes of containers makes them easier to stack and store. Ask parents to donate recyclable items.

- Plastic dishpans for completed work
- Plastic crates for file folders
- Copy paper boxes and box lids for storing writing paper on a tabletop
- Baskets for art supplies and manipulatives
- Vinyl place mats and shallow soda can cases (Trace the bottom of a container or tool onto the mat or box bottom to show where it belongs.)
- Detergent boxes (Paint, clip together with brads, and label with student names for storing work.)
- Plastic food storage containers with lids, such as frosting cans, for storing manipulatives
- Plastic shoebox-size storage boxes with lids
- Zippered freezer bags labeled with students' names for carrying supplies
- Large food cans from the cafeteria
- Plastic film containers for baby teeth and other uses

0-7682-2607-4 *Great Rooms! Grades K–1*

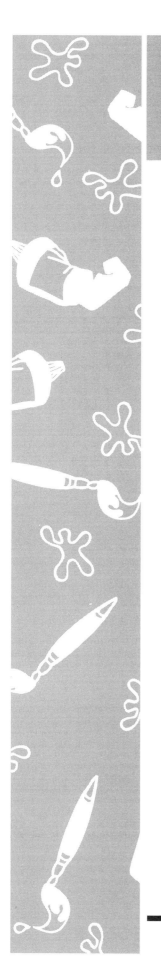

Organizing and Maintaining Supplies

Teacher Supplies Checklist

Here are must-have items for the efficient classroom:

Lesson plan book	Overhead projector pens
Record/Grade book	Permanent marker
Attendance roster	Highlighter pen
Teacher's guides for all texts	Crayons
Substitute folder	Glue sticks
Dictionary	Glue gun
Scissors	Paper clips
Stapler	Large binder clips
Staples	Small binder clips
Staple remover	Self-stick notes
Thumbtacks	File folders
Pins	Note pad
Ruler	Box of thank-you notes
Tape measure	Box of stationery
Yardstick	Reward stickers
Paper punch	Reward badges
Three-hole punch	Reward notes
Masking tape	Pocket apron
Transparent tape	Small bell
Pencils	Kitchen timer
Electric pencil sharpener	Clothes hangers for your closet
Erasers	Mirror for your closet
Pens	

0-7682-2607-4 *Great Rooms! Grades K–1*

Storage Solutions

A Dozen Classroom Storage Tips

- Store charts by clipping them to skirt hangers and hanging them in a closet. Cover with a cleaner's bag or trash bag and label the outside.

- Store large bulletin board pieces in trash bags hung from skirt hangers.

- Organize small bulletin board pieces and letters in manila envelopes. Label the envelope. Include a sketch of the bulletin board inside the envelope.

- Keep milk money or lunch money in plastic film containers labeled with children's names.

- Roll up number lines and bulletin board trim and store them in clean frosting cans with plastic lids.

- Use a cleaning supplies tote for often-needed teacher's supplies, such as stapler, scissors, and tape. It can be carried around the room as needed.

- Place yarn scraps, fabric pieces, buttons, and various odds and ends that have no home in a large coffee can with a lid at the art center for use in projects.

- Store headphones in zipper-lock plastic bags to keep the cords from tangling.

- Have children keep small loose items, such as pencils, erasers, and coins, in a plastic zipper-lock bag labeled with their name. The items will not roll around or get lost in a desk or cubbyhole.

- Store science and art center materials in plastic tubs with lids. Slide the tubs under a table for out-of-the-way storage.

- Get a large plastic laundry basket or tub for lunch boxes. Children can place their lunches in the tub when they enter in the morning.

- Place items you do not use anymore in the teacher's workroom with a sign that says *Free to a Good Home*. If they are not gone in a day, toss them away.

0-7682-2607-4 *Great Rooms! Grades K–1*

Building and Organizing a Classroom Library

Library Corner

A library corner is an important part of the kindergarten and first grade classroom. To make the corner inviting, you might include an area rug or carpet squares, pillows, a stuffed animal friend for the children to read to, a bean bag chair or child-size beach chair, and a green plant. Make sure the books are within easy reach on a shelf or bookcase. A book display rack allows books to be displayed with their covers out so children can see the inviting artwork.

Featured Books

Have a special area of the library corner where children can always look for featured books that you select from the public library or school library. The featured books can tie in with a curriculum topic you are currently studying. Make a simple sign on a sentence strip, for example, "Books About Spring," and tape it to the shelf.

Author, Author!

Choose an "Author of the Month" to feature in the library corner with several books on display. Read aloud the books during the month and discuss them. You might find a book poster or photo of the author to display along with the books. As a writing activity, invite the children to copy the author's name and the name of the book they liked best. Place an empty tissue box in the library corner. Have them place their papers in the box. When all votes are in, count them and announce the book title with the most votes.

Book Storage

If shelf space is limited for the classroom library, use baskets to hold books. You can also turn plastic crates on their sides and stand books in them.

© McGraw-Hill Children's Publishing

0-7682-2607-4 *Great Rooms! Grades K–1*

Building and Organizing a Classroom Library

Stocking the Library Corner

There are many ways to stock your classroom library with books. Yard sales, thrift stores, and library book sales are good places to find inexpensive books. Do you know any teachers who are retiring? They may be happy to have their books continue to be used in a classroom. Used bookstores often sell children's books at good prices. Ask parents to donate books their children no longer use. You can order or earn bonus books if your school has a student book-purchasing program. Borrow books from the public library, because some have extended loans for teachers. Rotate your supply of books, storing some away for a time and bringing out new ones.

Birthday Books

Suggest to parents that children can celebrate their birthdays by donating a new or used book to the classroom library. Provide bookplates to acknowledge the giver of each book. Write the child's name and place the bookplate at the front of the book. Be sure to read the book aloud to the class so everyone can say thank-you to the giver.

Music to Read By

Music can make the library corner even more inviting to young children. Include a tape player, headphones, and a tape of classical music for children to listen to as they read. Teach them proper handling and storage of the tape player.

Other Reading Materials

When it comes to stocking your library corner, don't stop at picture books. There are many types of reading materials that young children can read, enjoy, and learn from. Provide a wide variety of reading material to inspire a love of reading, such as poetry, children's magazines, books made by the entire class, big books, easy chapter books, charts written as a class, pop-up books, picture dictionaries, beginning dictionaries, book and tape combinations, books in other languages, maps, calendars, postcards and letters, menus, brochures, and catalogs.

© McGraw-Hill Children's Publishing

36

0-7682-2607-4 *Great Rooms! Grades K–1*

Classroom Library (cont.)

Library Categories

Many of the books in your classroom library will relate to topics and themes that you teach throughout the year. These books can be easily categorized and kept in a special basket or tub labeled with the current theme. Teach the children to return the books where they got them. Weekly classroom job assignments can include "Librarians"—two children in charge of putting the books in order during cleanup time.

— Creating Categories

There are many ways to organize books in a classroom library, for example, by curriculum themes or alphabetically by author or title. Even early grade classroom libraries can be organized by genre or subject. Place different colored stickers or tape on the book spines to indicate the category, such as blue for fiction, green for nonfiction, red for poetry, and yellow for reference. Make a color-coded chart and post it in the library corner for children to see. The books can be further categorized by placing all the books about pets together, all the biographies together, all the fairy tales together, and so on. In this way, children can learn that there are many ways to write about the same topic.

Critical Thinking

Promote critical thinking in your students by asking their help in categorizing new books. After reading a book aloud to the class, ask them to help you find the right place for it in the library corner. Is the book fiction or nonfiction? What color should it be? By discussing the book in this way, children will learn to think about a book's category. They will also learn how to locate books on a topic they are interested in.

Library Research

Demonstrate for children that the library can be used to investigate something of interest or to answer a question. When a question arises during the day, model using the books in the library corner to find the answer. You might say this: *That's a good question, Antwon, let's look it up in a book. What kind of book might tell us the answer? Where can we find it?* Children will learn how to investigate things they are eager to learn about on their own.

Miscellaneous Ideas for an Efficient Classroom

Student Mailboxes

Individual mailboxes for your students can help your classroom run efficiently. Papers to go home, letters to parents, book order forms, and reminders can automatically go into the child's mailbox during the day. One of the last things children do before leaving for the day is to empty their mailboxes. Mailboxes can be made from clean ice cream containers or half-gallon milk cartons. Ask parents to save them and wash them thoroughly. They can be stapled together with a heavy-duty stapler or attached together with brads. If using milk cartons, cover the outside with colorful adhesive-backed paper. This will also serve to hold them together. Covering individual ice cream containers with adhesive paper will make them sturdy. Label the individual mailboxes with each child's name or photo. To prevent congestion at the mailboxes at dismissal time, place banks of them in different areas of the classroom.

Play a Tune

Playing classical music as children enter and exit the classroom can set a calming tone. Studies have shown that classical music can enhance children's learning, so try playing some Bach or Mozart during work time as well. Make this recorded music an everyday soundtrack for your classroom.

Lost and Found

Place a large plastic tub labeled Lost and Found near the door to your room and close to the children's coat racks. Place things left behind in the tub. Parents and children will know exactly where to look for forgotten boots, mittens, shoes, and hats.

A Positive Place

Make your classroom a positive environment for learning. Set a positive tone in your classroom with the words you choose. Add commercial signs and posters with positive statements, or make your own using phrases that have inspired you to succeed. You'll find a positive attitude is catching!

0-7682-2607-4 *Great Rooms! Grades K–1*

Chapter 2: Classroom Management

Read this chapter to find out about:

- classroom rules
- discipline techniques
- rewards and incentives
- attention moves
- quieting signals
- documenting behavior
- communicating expectations to children, parents, and helpers

0-7682-2607-4 *Great Rooms! Grades K–1*

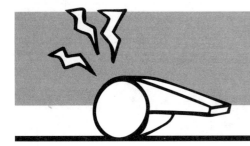

Classroom Rules

Rules for Success

It is a good idea to plan your classroom management goals before establishing the rules for your classroom. You want rules to help children achieve success and to provide a positive atmosphere for learning. For kindergarten and first grade classrooms it is wise to minimize the number of rules children must remember. Introduce classroom rules gradually throughout the first week of school, and reinforce them regularly with discussion and role-playing. Write the rules on a chart and post it in a prominent spot.

> ### Rules for Our Class
> **Show respect for others.**
>
> **Show respect for school things.**
>
> **Do your work.**
>
> **Be a listener.**
>
> **Be polite.**

Puppets Follow the Rules

Puppets capture children's attention and are a good way to introduce, reinforce, and demonstrate how to follow the rules. Use hand puppets to role-play situations, such as staying on task and following directions, and to demonstrate what is considered tattling and what is not.

A Golden Rule

The Golden Rule, *Treat others as you would like to be treated*, will give children a behavior guideline for almost any situation that arises. Post a sign or chart with this rule on it. Discuss its meaning and give your students an opportunity to tell how it can be applied, using the stories below. Throughout the school day, pause to point out student behavior that illustrates the Golden Rule.

Story 1: Vanessa dropped her school lunch ticket. Marlie sees the ticket on the ground. What should Marlie do?

Story 2: Reese accidentally bumped into Matt when Matt was drawing. Now Matt's picture has a big line across it. What can Reese do?

Story 3: After the blue group has left the art center, Gabe sees scraps of paper on the floor. What can he do?

 0-7682-2607-4 *Great Rooms! Grades K–1*

Discipline Techniques

Classroom Discipline

It is important to teach the type of behavior you wish your students to exhibit in class. Children do not automatically know how to listen or how to put things away properly. It may seem time-consuming, but taking the time to teach certain things will save time later. With young children, start with the very basics of how to work quietly, how to stand and walk in a line, how to move between learning centers, when not to interrupt the teacher, and what to do when work is finished. Teach specific lessons in each of the behaviors to make sure that your students understand your expectations.

Determining Consequences

It is important to let children know that improper behavior has consequences. Let them know what the consequences will be. An appropriate consequence might be time out from the activity at hand. Another consequence could be losing a classroom privilege the child enjoys, such as erasing the board, listening to a music tape, or going out to recess.

Helpful Tips—A-B-Cs

When disciplining children keep these tips in mind:

- Address the situation instead of judging the child's character.
- Be calm and matter-of-fact.
- Children need guidance not criticism.
- Stop misbehavior by showing you are willing to help. Some children may not ask for help when they need it.

Thank You

One way to acknowledge proper student behavior is with the simple words "thank you." Acknowledging that children are meeting behavioral expectations will reinforce their behavior and encourage others to follow suit. For example, instead of requesting over and over that everyone take their seats, a simple "Thank you for taking your seat" can be very effective. Modeling appreciation and respect for your students is a good way to inspire them to similar behavior.

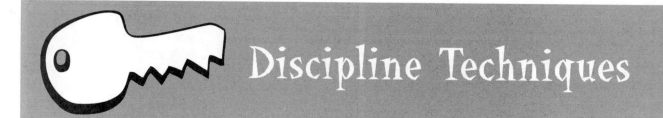

Discipline Techniques

Peaceable Solutions

Encourage a peaceful classroom by teaching children ways to settle their difficulties without fighting. Tell the children the Aesop fable of *The North Wind and the Sun*. This story illustrates that the use of gentleness and persuasion is more effective than force. Use the reproducible pictures on page 43 to trace and cut out felt characters for your flannelboard. Use the felt pieces to illustrate the story as you tell it. Make copies of the page for the children to color, cut out, and glue onto drawing paper after they have heard you tell the story. Have them add scenery and details to their picture and display them throughout the room.

"The North Wind and the Sun"
By Aesop

Once upon a time ago, the Wind and the Sun were having a disagreement. "I'm more powerful than you, and can prove it," the Wind bellowed. This made the Sun mad. While they were arguing, a traveler passed by, all wrapped up in a cloak. "Let's have a contest to see who is stronger," proposed the Sun. "Whoever can remove the Traveler's cloak will be the strongest." The Wind agreed and in no time at all began to blow an icy blast against the Traveler. The Traveler shivered and wrapped his cloak tight around him. The more the cold wind blew, the tighter he held his cloak. The angry Wind could not remove the coat. Now it was the Sun's turn. He began to shine. The Traveler felt warm in the Sun's gentle rays. He began to unbutton his cloak. Before long, the Sun's rays became warmer and warmer. As the Sun continued to shine, the Traveler took off his cloak and sat down in the shade of a big tree to cool off. The Wind had to admit that the sun was the stronger.

Gentleness can do what force cannot.

The North Wind and the Sun By Aesop

Gentleness can do what force cannot.

0-7682-2607-4 *Great Rooms! Grades K–1*

Children Making Choices

Help children understand that they can make choices about their own behavior. For example, if a child is disturbing others during group work, you can offer them a choice by saying this: *You are making it difficult for others to listen to directions. Would you like to stay with the group while we make our puppets or go back to your seat? Show me what you need to do if you want to stay.*

Classroom Atmosphere

Establishing a warm and accepting atmosphere in the kindergarten and first grade classroom will help to circumvent behavioral issues. Help the children feel a sense of belonging and control by giving them a say and allowing them to make decisions. You can do this by structuring their choices. For example, have the class choose which of two stories you will read aloud first, or allow them to decide which of two assignments they will complete first. On some assignments, have the children choose their own work partner.

Tattling 101

Sometimes children tattle without expecting intervention from the teacher. They may just feel the need for attention. Look for ways to give these children positive attention at other times by reinforcing their proper behavior. This may take away some of their need to tattle.

Purposeful Writing

Encourage children to solve their own problems with a writing exercise. Instruct children who are able to write to do just that—have both parties in a dispute write down what happened. Review their notes at a later time, and then call them together to tell you how they can resolve it. Drawing a picture of a positive resolution is also positive encouragement.

Discipline Techniques

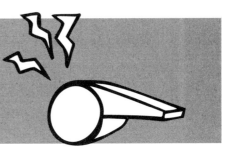

Taking Responsibility

If children tattle because they cannot resolve their differences or conflicts with other children on their own, it is a good idea to spend time discussing strategies for solving problems. Take time in a class meeting to role-play situations. Ask the children to contribute their ideas and words that might be used. Make a chart list together. Tell the children to try two of the ideas on the list before they come to you with a problem. On subsequent days, revisit the list and ask the children which ones worked. Have them add new suggestions to the list. Giving children the tools to settle their conflicts will reduce the number of times you hear such things as "Teacher, Alexa took my blue crayon."

Solving Problems

- Ask politely.
- Tell the person how you feel.
- Apologize.
- Take three deep breaths.

- Cool down, then talk.
- Tell the person to stop.
- Walk away.
- Try something else.

Is It Reporting or Tattling?

Help children learn when it is important to report something to the teacher and when they should try to resolve a problem themselves. Discuss some of the things children tattle about in school. Help them see that if something is dangerous or harmful to a person or to property, they should tell the teacher immediately. Explain that it is a helpful and responsible thing to do. Discuss examples, such as reporting someone damaging playground equipment or reporting that someone fell and is hurt.

Community in the Classroom

Promote a sense of community to minimize behavior problems in the classroom. Introduce a secret pal activity. Have each child pull the name of a classmate from a hat. Tell the children they must keep the name a secret. During the week they must find a way to share something with their secret pal, without letting on that they picked their name. At the end of the week, ask the children to guess who had their names. Have them tell what their secret pal shared.

Rewards and Incentives

You Are a Sunbeam!

Encourage positive behavior in your students with this simple incentive activity. Write "You Are a Sunbeam" in an area of the whiteboard. Designate this area for the names of students whom you observe behaving positively. Tell the children that during the school day, you will record the names of those students whom you catch following the rules, being helpful, and so on. Each school day, write several names on the board. The next day, give them each a Sunbeam Note from page 47 that says *You Are a Sunbeam! Thank you for making our classroom brighter.* The children can keep their notes in a zipper-lock sandwich bag until they have collected a number that you specify. They can then redeem their Sunbeam Notes for a reward from a special box of free and inexpensive items you collect, such as erasers, pencils, notepads, and other small favors.

Teddy Bears on Parade

To reward positive behavior, give a child an opportunity to keep the class mascot—a small stuffed bear or other animal—at their seat during a lesson or work time. Do this once a day and keep track on a class list of who has had a turn, so everyone will have an opportunity.

Flying High

Make a copy of the *Flying High* kite from page 48 on colored paper for each child. Post the kites on a length of bulletin board paper on a wall or the back of a bookcase with the title "Up We Go." Reserve some special stickers for children to earn. Explain that they can decorate their kites by earning stickers. Give stickers as rewards for following rules and procedures, being a friend, doing an act of kindness, or doing their best work. Allow the children to place the stickers on their kites when they earn them.

Sunbeam Notes

Name_____

YOU ARE A SUNBEAM!

Thank you for making our classroom brighter.

Name_____

YOU ARE A SUNBEAM!

Thank you for making our classroom brighter.

Name_____

YOU ARE A SUNBEAM!

Thank you for making our classroom brighter.

Name_____

YOU ARE A SUNBEAM!

Thank you for making our classroom brighter.

Name_____

YOU ARE A SUNBEAM!

Thank you for making our classroom brighter.

Name_____

YOU ARE A SUNBEAM!

Thank you for making our classroom brighter.

0-7682-2607-4 *Great Rooms! Grades K–1*

Name_____ Date_____

Flying High

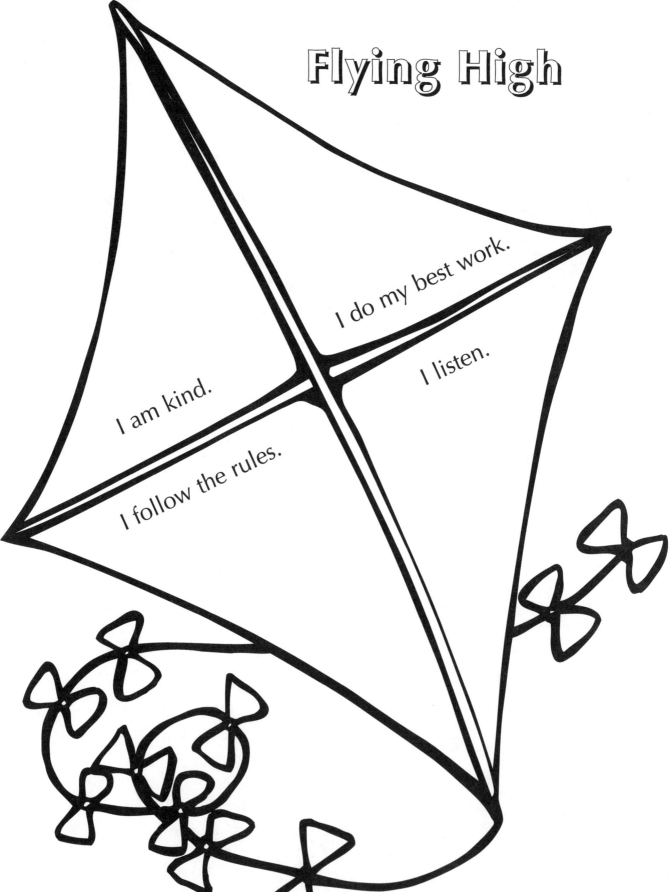

I do my best work.

I listen.

I am kind.

I follow the rules.

48

0-7682-2607-4 Great Rooms! Grades K–1

Rewards and Incentives

Respect Is Catching!

Encourage the children in your class to show respect for others and for the classroom environment. Play a game of catching them at showing respect. Explain that in this game, the children must be on the lookout for classmates who show respect in something they say or do. If they "catch" someone showing respect, they can give that person a token. Make a copy of page 50 on heavy paper for each child. Have the children write their name on each of the five tokens and cut them out. Give them a zipper-lock sandwich bag with their name on it for their tokens. Explain that the object of the game is to give away all of their tokens in one week. They will also receive tokens when they show respect. Make several extra tokens for yourself, so you can make sure that everyone receives some during the week. Take a few minutes at the end of each day to ask who received a token that day. Have someone who gave away a token tell to whom they gave it and how that person showed respect.

Showing Respect

- Help someone clean up.
- Tell someone you like his or her drawing.
- Let someone get a drink first.
- Hold the door open for someone.
- Share a book with someone.

Wristband Rewards

Children will be proud to wear a wristband that rewards their best efforts. Make copies of page 51 on heavy paper and cut them into thirds. Keep a supply of wristbands handy. When your students earn a wristband for doing their best work, they can color and cut it out. You can tape or staple it securely around their wrist.

Instant Rewards and Rewards Checklist

Keep a set of little awards on hand to instantly reward children's work or behavior. Make copies of page 52, cut apart the awards, and store them in an envelope so they are readily available. Then use the Rewards Checklist on page 53 to keep track of the rewards and incentives you give out. It will tell you at a glance where you need to focus attention so every child receives reinforcement for positive behavior. If desired, write dates in the empty column headings (weeks or months). Simply make a checkmark in a box each time you reward a student.

Catch Respect!

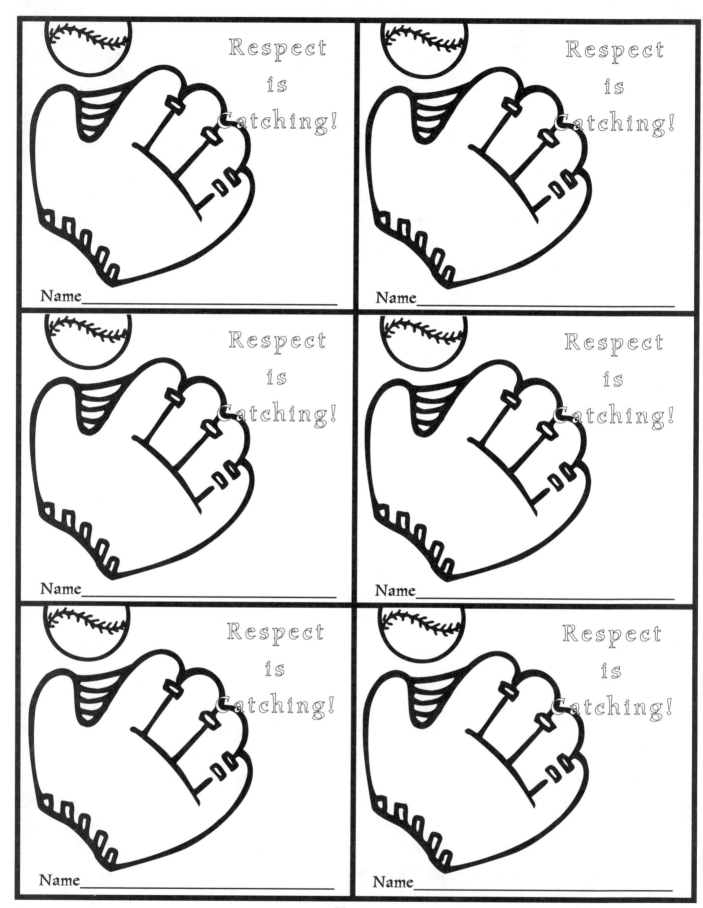

Respect is Catching!

Name_____

Respect is Catching!

Name_____

Respect is Catching!

Name_____

Respect is Catching!

Name_____

Respect is Catching!

Name_____

Respect is Catching!

Name_____

0-7682-2607-4 *Great Rooms! Grades K–1*

Wristband Rewards

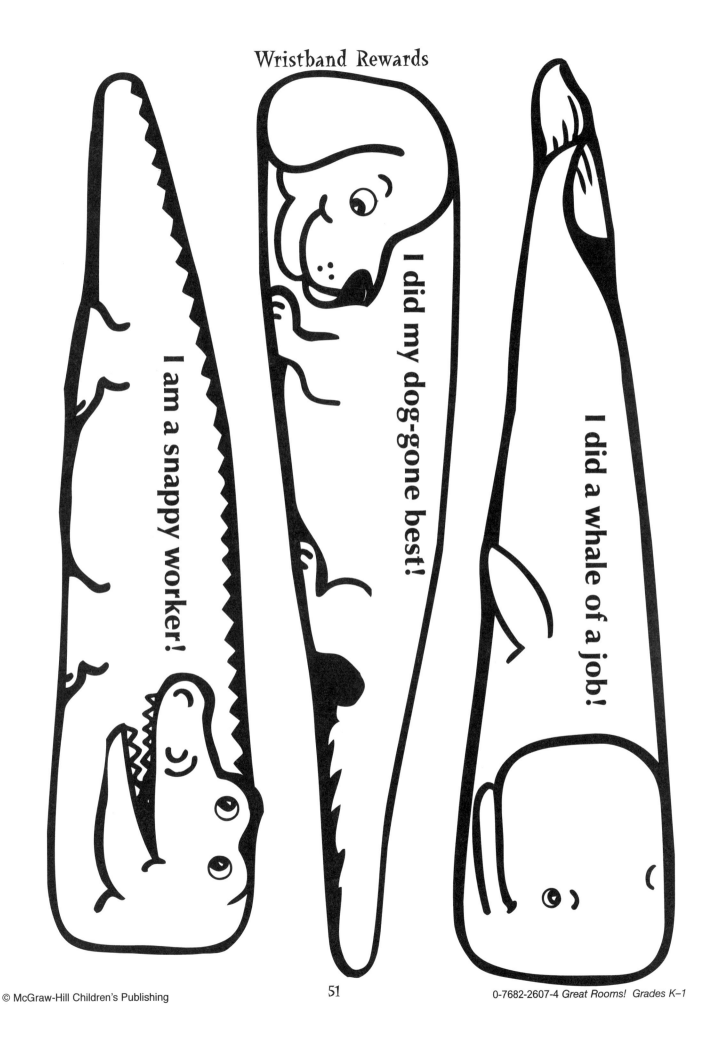

I am a snappy worker!

I did my dog-gone best!

I did a whale of a job!

0-7682-2607-4 *Great Rooms! Grades K–1*

0-7682-2607-4 *Great Rooms! Grades K–1*

Rewards Checklist

Teacher _____ Grade _____ Room _____

Student's Name											
1.											
2.											
3.											
4.											
5.											
6.											
7.											
8.											
9.											
10.											
11.											
12.											
13.											
14.											
15.											
16.											
17.											
18.											
19.											
20.											
21.											
22.											
23.											
24.											
25.											
26.											
27.											
28.											
29.											
30.											
31.											
32.											

0-7682-2607-4 *Great Rooms! Grades K–1*

Rewards and Incentives

Making Praise Work

Make your praise a comment on the child's actions rather than a comment on them as a person. Children respond best to praise when it speaks specifically to what they did. Effective praise includes encouragement to repeat the positive actions. For example, you might say, *Thank you for writing your name in your best handwriting, José. Please do that again with next week's words.*

Praise with Pizzazz

Vary your comments when praising children for their behavior and work efforts. Try some of the phrases listed here to add pizzazz to your remarks and to give children a boost of confidence.

Delightful	*You're a word wizard*	*I'm proud of you*
One-of-a-kind	*You're a mathemagician*	*Bravo*
Wow, I like this!	*Blue ribbon winner*	*Lovely*
Hooray	*Frame this!*	*Hot dog!*
Three cheers!	*You were really thinking*	*Thank you*
Awesome work	*Good for you*	*Your best yet!*

No-Cost Rewards

It is not always necessary for teachers to spend out-of-pocket for rewards. Make a list of privileges and activities that can serve as rewards for deserving students. Keep your list handy for instant rewards. For example, it's fun to promise "a handshake and a pat on the back" and then deliver it with a smile when the student completes the task. Other rewards might be reading a book to a younger child, having free time to draw or play with clay, sitting at the teacher's desk to do an assignment, drawing on the board, using rubber stamps, or staying in with a friend at recess.

Attention Moves

What Are You Communicating?

When you want to be sure a child or a group of children get the message you are communicating, remember to move toward them instead of speaking to them from across the room. Establish eye contact and use a soft voice to hold their attention.

Have a Seat

Young children who have difficulty sitting still or paying attention for any length of time can be seated near the teacher during story time or circle time activities. This makes it easier to keep eye contact. Seating children next to someone who can model proper behavior is another technique for minimizing disruption. Potentially distractive students can also be placed near the front of the line so they are close to the teacher.

Stand By

Some children just naturally need to move more than others, but their energy can disrupt the lesson at hand. By walking over to a child and placing a gentle hand on her shoulder, you can give a silent reminder to calm down. After a few repetitions, the child will recognize what you are communicating with a gesture.

Teacher Placement

While working with a group of children, you want to be able to see the rest of the class and monitor them. Place your table for small group work at the front of the class. Your chair can face the group, and beyond them, the rest of the class. The children in the group will be sitting with their backs to the class to minimize distractions. The class will be able to see the group at work, modeling positive behavior.

0-7682-2607-4 *Great Rooms! Grades K–1*

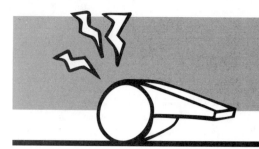

Quieting Signals

Clap Like Me

To gain children's attention in a group and quiet them for further instructions, it is not necessary to say a word. Teach them that when they hear you clap a rhythm, they should stop what they are doing and answer you by clapping the same rhythm. Echoing you brings all their activity—both physical and mental—into focus. This is a cue for them to stop and listen. Invent rhythms or use some of the following:

1-2, 1-2-3 (clap-clap-pause-clap-clap-clap)

1-2-3, 1-2-3

1-2, 1-2, 1-2

1-2-3-4, 1-2

Save Your Voice

Quieting signals are an effective management tool in the early grade classroom. First, explain to your students the behaviors you wish to see when they hear a signal. You may want them to look at you, freeze in place, and stop all talking. Second, demonstrate by giving the signal and having a child show what to do. Repeat with other volunteers. Have the entire class practice it. Finally, begin your next activity, but let the children know you are going to give the signal again. After a minute or two, give the signal. Give the signal only once and do not speak, just wait for the children to give you their attention. Then, compliment them and review what they did. Practice in this way a few times to reinforce the procedure. Here are some signals to choose from:

- Bell
- Kitchen timer
- Music box
- Rain stick
- Triangle
- Chimes

- Lights off and on
- Musical recording
- Song
- Give me five. (Raise hand and silently or verbally count to five by showing one finger, two fingers, etc.)

Quieting Signals

Lower and Lower

Have you ever found yourself raising the volume of your voice to be heard above the class? The louder you get, the louder they seem to get. If you find yourself in this situation, try having some fun. Simply stop and lower your voice to a whisper. The children nearest you will catch on first, and if you keep it to a whisper, the students will quiet the others for you.

Make Mine Music

If you have a piano in your classroom, select a favorite song to teach the children. Use the first few bars of the song as a signal for cleanup time at the end of the school day. Explain that when they hear the music begin, they must start putting things away and tending to their classroom jobs. Singing can make work lighter! Continue the song with the children singing along as they clean up. For some imaginative fun, you might select a sea chantey or other work song from a collection of folk songs.

— Rhyme for a Reason

Teaching your students a rhyme with movements will draw their attention and help them to get ready to listen.

> Hands up high, I touch the sky. (*Raise hands in the air.*)
>
> Hands on shoulders, my oh my. (*Hands on shoulders.*)
>
> Hands together, I bring them down, (*Fold hands.*)
>
> Into my lap without a sound. (*All talking stops.*)
>
> —*Barbara Allman*

Snap to It

Most children find it an entertaining challenge to learn to snap their fingers. When you want to get their attention, begin snapping your fingers to a slow, steady beat and have them try to keep on the beat with you. Use this as a signal for them to take a seat, line up, or whatever you wish.

    0-7682-2607-4 *Great Rooms! Grades K–1*

Documenting Behavior

Keep a List Handy

Post a list of names for each reading or math group near the worktable so it is handy while you are working with groups. Make enough copies so that you will have a new list each week. Explain to the children that you will make a checkmark next to the name of anyone who does not follow the rules or procedures during their group's time. At the end of the week, the group with the fewest checkmarks will earn a classroom privilege of your choice, such as lining up first, passing out the snacks, or playing a learning lotto game. Date and keep your lists to document students' behavior during small group time.

Tiger Time

Make a behavior or a skills chart for children to keep track of their own success at following the rules. Title it "Tiger Time." Use library pockets and a tiger bookmark (page 59) for each child. Label each pocket with a child's name. Put numbered bookmarks in a basket next to the chart. Place a tiger bookmark in the pocket of each child who follows the rules, exhibits a desired character trait, or masters a skill such as cutting with scissors or tying their shoes.

To use the *Tiger Time Record Sheet*, make a master copy of the page with children's names. Copy it to make a sheet for each week. The sheet is a handy record when reporting to parents or assessing skills. You can use this system with a box of small rewards or incentives. At the end of the week, allow children who have obtained several tigers to select an item from the box.

Tiger Time

0-7682-2607-4 *Great Rooms! Grades K–1*

Tiger Time

Week of _____   Skill_____

Student's Name	Mon.	Tues.	Wed.	Thurs.	Fri.
1.					
2.					
3.					
4.					
5.					
6.					
7.					
8.					
9.					
10.					
11.					
12.					
13.					
14.					
15.					
16.					
17.					
18.					
19.					
20.					
21.					
22.					
23.					
24.					
25.					
26.					
27.					
28.					
29.					
30.					
31.					
32.					

0-7682-2607-4 *Great Rooms! Grades K–1*

Communicating Expectations to All

I'm Finished, What Do I Do Now?

Be sure children know what is expected of them when they have finished an assignment, so they do not have to interrupt you to ask, "What do I do now?" Make a list on chart paper of the activities children may do when they have finished their work and have extra time. For pre-readers, draw symbols representing the activities and be sure they know how to read them. Clip clothespins to the chart to indicate the activities that are available that day. Children will gain confidence when they can make choices and manage their own time.

Things to Do on My Own:

Pocket chart story

Math game

Puzzle

Word hunt

Read the Word Wall

Write numbers

Practice handwriting

Rules for Our Class

Let parents know you have established and discussed rules for proper classroom behavior. Send home a note explaining this and listing the rules. See page 62 for a letter that can be completed by you and then copied. Ask parents to discuss the rules with their child. Request that both parent and child sign the letter and return it to school. Keep the letter on file to be used when needed to remind the children of their commitment to follow the rules.

Home Communication Log

Use the *Home Communication Log* (page 64) to make notes on your phone conversations, in-person meetings, and written communications with parents. A log makes it easy to record the date and pertinent information discussed, as well as any follow-up or response.

_____
Date

Dear Family,

In school, we have discussed the importance of rules to help everyone learn and do his or her best. Below is a list of rules for our class. Please take a few moments to read and discuss them with your child. Then, please sign this paper and have your child return it to school. Thank you for your cooperation.

Sincerely,

_____
Teacher

Our Class Rules

_____
_____
_____
_____
_____
_____
_____

Family member's signature: _____

Student's signature: _____

0-7682-2607-4 _Great Rooms! Grades K–1_

Emergency Contact Form

Child's Name: _____

Date of Birth: _____

Allergies or Medical Conditions: _____

_____

Mother's Contact Information

Name of Mother/Guardian: _____

Home Address: _____

Daytime Phone: _____ Evening Phone: _____

Cell Phone: _____

Father's Contact Information

Name of Father/Guardian: _____

Home Address: _____

Daytime Phone: _____ Evening Phone: _____

Cell Phone: _____

Other Emergency Contact: _____

Relation to student: _____

Daytime Phone: _____ Evening Phone: _____

Cell Phone: _____

Physician's Name: _____

Physician's Phone: _____

© McGraw-Hill Children's Publishing

0-7682-2607-4 *Great Rooms! Grades K–1*

Home Communication Log

Child's Name: _____

Date: _____

Subject: _____

Person contacted: _____ How contacted: _____

Response _____

_____

Follow-Up _____

_____

Date: _____

Subject: _____

Person contacted: _____ How contacted: _____

Response _____

_____

Follow-Up _____

_____

Date: _____

Subject: _____

Person contacted: _____ How contacted: _____

Response _____

_____

Follow-Up _____

_____

0-7682-2607-4 *Great Rooms! Grades K–1*

Communication

Helper Box

Place a plastic tub, basket, or box in a convenient spot where you can put filing, copying, cutting, assembling, and decorating jobs for your parent volunteers or other helpers. Keep a pad of paper in the tub for jotting down quick instructions and numbering the jobs in order of priority. Ask your helpers to check the tub first, then to see you with any questions or for further instructions.

Notes Home

It is important to reinforce positive behavior with home communication. Use the notes on page 66 to make sure that each child receives a positive note to take home once a month. Use your grade book or a copy of your class list to keep track of children who receive a note.

Reminder Notes

Children often need a note to take home as a reminder to bring in a library book, replenish supplies, bring in a snack, and so on. Duplicate multiple sheets of the reminders on page 67, have an aide cut them apart, and store them in an index card box with dividers or in a drawer divider tray. You can hand them out to children as needed as they leave to go home. As children gain confidence, send them to the tray to get a reminder, write their name on it, and put it in their homework folder to take home.

In and Out

Keep clear plastic In and Out boxes near the door to the classroom. Show your students where to place notes from home (the In box) when they enter in the morning. Use the Out box to hold notes you want to send home. Appoint a child to be the Note Monitor. Show that child how to check the In and Out boxes in the morning and at dismissal.

Classroom Web Site

Keep the parents of your students informed about what is happening in your classroom by creating a Web site. Check with your school or district on how to do this as part of the school's site. Display the children's artwork on a home page, or explain homework assignments. Include a link with your school e-mail address. Encourage family members to send messages to their child via your e-mail address, which you can read and pass along.

0-7682-2607-4 Great Rooms! Grades K–1

Something to Cheer About!

Dear _____,

I noticed that _____ did really well

in _____ today. Your child showed an amazing ability to

_____.

Please congratulate your child on this positive effort!

Sincerely,

_____

Something to Cheer About!

Dear _____,

I noticed that _____ did really well

in _____ today. Your child showed an amazing ability to

_____.

Please congratulate your child on this positive effort!

Sincerely,

_____

0-7682-2607-4 *Great Rooms! Grades K–1*

Name _____ Date _____

Reminder Note

☐ Library Tomorrow

☐ Test Tomorrow

☐ I need to remember my homework!

☐ Don't Forget _____

☐ I need more _____

☐ Please Remember Permission Slip

Name _____ Date _____

Reminder Note

☐ Library Tomorrow

☐ Test Tomorrow

☐ I need to remember my homework!

☐ Don't Forget _____

☐ I need more _____

☐ Please Remember Permission Slip

Chapter 3: Establishing Routines

Read this chapter to find out about:

- morning routines
- attendance and absences
- lunch count
- circle time
- lining up
- asking for assistance
- classroom helpers
- dismissal
- substitute teachers

Hello, Have a Nice Day!

A consistent morning routine as children enter the classroom will make them feel comfortable and confident. At the beginning of the year, be sure that the children know where to hang outerwear and put away their things. You may want to label the coat hooks so each child knows where his things go. Provide a large plastic tub or laundry basket near the coat rack for lunch boxes. As winter approaches, send home a reminder asking parents to label both boots on the inside, as many children wear the same style and size. You can provide clip-on clothespins with the children's names on them as well. Have children clip their boots together before placing them in the proper location.

Morning Routines

A Place for Me

On the first day of school, give the children a sticker when they enter the classroom. Have them find the matching sticker on the floor and sit there for the morning meeting. If you wish to assign places in the circle once you get to know the children, use colorful plastic tape with their names written on it to mark their places.

— Sing Along

A good way to start the day is with a favorite song or songs. Singing together can help establish camaraderie and a sense of community in the classroom. Choose songs that emphasize caring, such as "One Light, One Sun" by Raffi and "This Land Is Your Land" by Woody Guthrie, as well as traditional songs, such as "Playmate," "The More We Get Together," and "There's a Little Wheel A-Turning." Write the words on chart paper so you or a child can track them with a "magic wand" or other pointer as everybody sings along. Add to the charts as you teach new songs. By singing and seeing the song charts daily, the children will add to their sight vocabulary.

The More We Get Together

The more we get together, together, together,

The more we get together, the happier we'll be!

For my friend is your friend, and your friend is my friend;

The more we get together, the happier are we!

Morning Routines

Morning Message

In preparation for the school day, write a two- or three-sentence morning message on chart paper. Your message can state what will be happening in school today, who is coming to visit, what projects the class will work on, comments about yesterday's activities, and so on. The children will eagerly look for the message to find out what is new when they enter the classroom each morning. As they become more proficient at reading the message, include a simple question for the children to answer. This can be their first assignment for the day. You might also write instructions, such as what supplies to have at their desk for the first activity. Read the morning message together when everyone has gathered on the rug. Use the vocabulary in the message to teach quick lessons in letter sounds, punctuation, rhyming words, and word families.

Question of the Day

Write a question on a sentence strip before class begins each day. Structure the question so it requires a simple yes or no, or other one-word answer. For example, *Have you ever seen a live giraffe?* or *How many sisters do you have?* Provide a large sheet of paper for children to write their name and answer. If it is a yes or no question, draw two columns on the paper, one labeled Yes and the other No. Post the question on an easel or bulletin board. The children can sign their name in one of the columns to indicate their answer. Each week, assign two children the classroom job of making sure that everyone answers the question when they enter the classroom. Teach these two Questioners the procedure you want the class to follow. The Questioners should have a pen or pencil. They should read the question to you and record their answer. They can help others read the question and make sure that everyone has a turn to answer. During circle time, read the question of the day together and discuss the results of the poll.

Routines (cont.)

Reading Record

Include purposeful reading and writing activities in the morning routine whenever possible. One way to do this is to have the children contribute to a display of books read. Each week assign a student or two the job of Book Recorder. (See page 72 for a form.) Place books you have read aloud in a special box. During the morning routine, the Book Recorder takes the books read the previous day, records their title and author, and signs their name on the form. Post the forms on a bulletin board or hall display to show what the class is reading. Or, assemble them into a booklet for the classroom library. Children will enjoy browsing through the lists of books they have heard and read together.

Please Sign In

Keep an attendance register in your classroom for children to check each morning. This is one way to give children a purposeful reading experience. Enlarge the names and boxes. Before the children arrive each day, write the date at the top of the page. Teach the children to be responsible for checking in next to their names as part of their morning routine—putting away their things, turning in notes, and so on. With this sheet, you will be able to tell at a glance who is absent.

Attendance and Lunch Tags

This easy method of keeping track of attendance and lunch count works with a whiteboard that accepts magnets. Make an attendance tag for each child by writing the name on a small poster board rectangle. Laminate the tags, and attach a small piece of magnetic strip to the back of each one. Create and label columns on the board such as these: *Names, Milk, Hot Lunch, Cold Lunch*. Place all tags in the Names column. Teach the children that when they enter in the morning, they move their magnet to the column that indicates their lunch preference. You will be able to readily identify absent students by looking at which tags have not been moved. Have a helper return all the tags to the Names column at the end of the day.

Absent Work Folders

When a child is absent from class, pull out a file folder and write their name on it. Place the folder at the child's table and ask another child who sits near them to place today's papers in the folder. Also, have the child copy any board assignments to be completed. Finally, reward your helper by letting them use rubber stamps to decorate the folder.

0-7682-2607-4 *Great Rooms! Grades K–1*

Books We Read Together

Title _____

Author _____

Date _____

Title _____

Author _____

Name _____

0-7682-2607-4 *Great Rooms! Grades K–1*

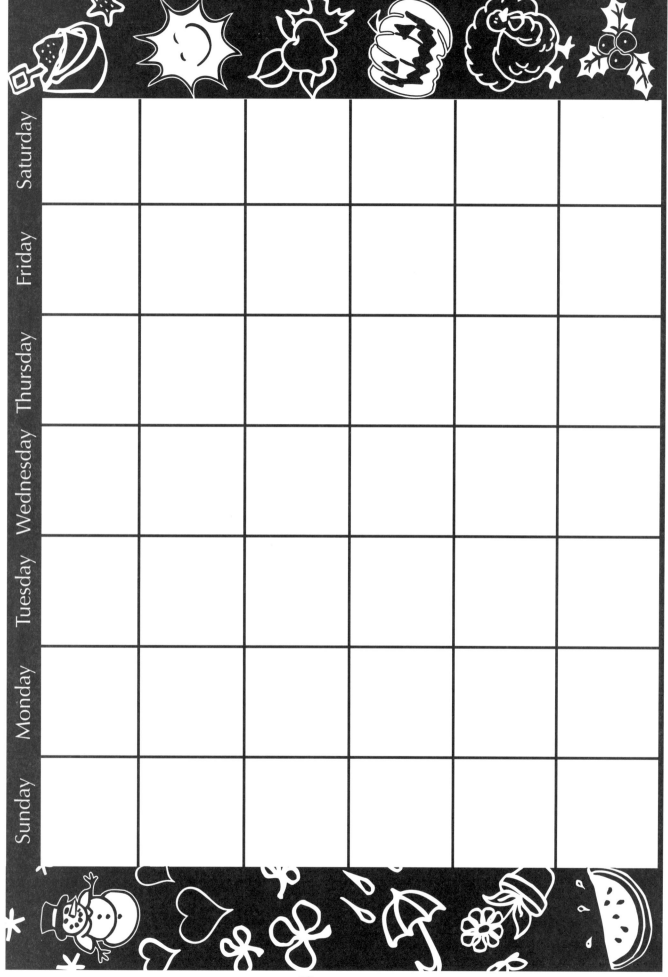

Month of:

Sunday	Monday	Tuesday	Wednesday	Thursday	Friday	Saturday

0-7682-2607-4 *Great Rooms! Grades K–1*

Circle Time

Today's Topic

Taking time for verbal sharing helps establish a community in the classroom and develops children's oral and listening skills. Each week, assign a child the job of Morning Meeting Leader. Use different topics to set the tone for the meeting. Have the leader state the topic each day and call on the children, going around the circle. Allow the children to contribute or pass. Topics may include the following:

Today's News—Children tell about something important to them today. (*My dad is going to show me how to ride my two-wheeler.*)

Greeters—In turn, children greet the person next to them and say something positive. (Good morning, Alex. I'm glad you're here today.)

Sharing Day—Establish one day a week as sharing day. The leader calls on those who brought something to show the class.

Today's Plan—Children tell one thing they are looking forward to doing in school today.

Yesterday in Review—Children tell one thing that happened yesterday in or out of school.

Show and Tell

Give each child an opportunity to bring something in for show and tell. Limit the activity to only a certain number of children on a given day. Instruct the children to bring their item in a brown paper bag. Have parents help them write three clues about their item. Sending home a note with instructions will help the children remember their day and what they are to do. When it is their turn to share, have the children read their clues and allow the class to guess what is inside their bag.

Sharing Schedule

Set up a schedule for sharing time. Assign a day of the week for each child to bring in something to "show and tell" if they wish. Keep the same schedule all year, so that children will know their day is Tuesday, for example. Teach the children to recognize the difference between a comment and a question. When the presenter is done sharing, the other members of the class may raise their hands if they have a comment or question. Teach the children to preface a comment with the phrase, "I have a comment." If they have a question, they should say, "I have a question."

0-7682-2607-4 *Great Rooms! Grades K–1*

Circle Time

How Do You Say That in Japanese?

Have children greet each other each morning during circle time. Teach a variety of words and ways to greet someone. Children can shake hands, wave hello, bow, and curtsey. Can they think of other movements? Ask parents if they can teach the class greetings in other languages. Sing a song, such as "Hello to All the Children of the World" from *Wee Sing Around the World* (Price Stern Sloan, 1994). It includes these greetings:

Bonjour (French) good day

Buenos días (Spanish) good day

G'day (Australia) good day

Guten Tag (German) good day

Kon nichi wa (Japanese) hello

Ciao (Italian) hi, goodbye

Shalom (Hebrew) hello, goodbye, peace

Dobrey Dyen (Russian) good day

School Year Time Line

Make a simple time line of the days in the school year using a long strip of adding machine tape the length of the wall. Label it with the numbers from 1 to 180 (or however many days are in your school year). Post it in a place and at a level where children can reach it. Each day during circle time have a student mark off the number for that day on the time line.

Calendar Board Patterns

Dedicating a bulletin board in the classroom to a monthly calendar provides opportunities for many types of literacy and math activities. At the beginning of the year, you can lead children in calendar activities, introducing them one at a time. Later in the year you can appoint a child to lead the group while you participate. Use a simple activity that teaches patterning. Make the calendar numbers for the month at least on two different paper shapes—for example, a turkey and a Pilgrim hat. Write the numbers on the shapes so that when they are pinned to the calendar grid they will make a visual pattern, such as turkey, turkey, hat, turkey, turkey, hat, and so on. Before each number is placed on the calendar, have the children predict what shape it will be.

© McGraw-Hill Children's Publishing

75

0-7682-2607-4 *Great Rooms! Grades K–1*

Circle Time

What Day Is Today?

After placing a number on the calendar grid, ask questions such as the following: What day is today? *If today is Friday, what day was yesterday? If today is Friday, what day is tomorrow?* These questions will help children acquire a sense of time. Use the calendar provided on page 73.

Seasons of the Year

Display the names of the four seasons along with representative pictures of each one on the calendar board. Include a mention of the current season each time you address the calendar. Make a paper arrow from sturdy paper and label it *The season is*. Move the arrow when the seasons change and talk about some of the signs of the season.

Graphing the Weather

A daily look at a weather graph during circle time familiarizes children with graphing techniques as well as heightens their awareness of changes in the weather. Use the reproducible categories and pictures on pages 77–78 to make a bulletin board pictograph. Write the title "Our Weather Graph" on a sentence strip and staple it to the board at the top. Color, cut out, and laminate the categories from page 77 and staple them in a row at the bottom of the board. Make several copies of page 78 and cut apart the pictures. Each day, have the children choose a picture that best represents the weather and place it on the board in the proper column. Discuss the growth of the graph and draw comparisons among the number of days in each column. Make copies of page 79 so that each child can have a bar graph that corresponds to the class pictograph. The children can be responsible for coloring in the matching space on their graph each day.

0-7682-2607-4 *Great Rooms! Grades K–1*

RAINY	**CLOUDY**
SNOWY	**WINDY**
FOGGY	**SUNNY**
HOT	**COLD**

0-7682-2607-4 *Great Rooms! Grades K–1*

Graphing the Weather—Categories

0-7682-2607-4 *Great Rooms! Grades K–1*

Name _____

My Weather Graph

Beginning Date_____ Ending Date_____

Number of Days

10							
9							
8							
7							
6							
5							
4							
3							
2							
1							

Sunny   Rainy   Foggy   Cold   Hot   Windy   Snowy   Cloudy

0-7682-2607-4 *Great Rooms! Grades K–1*

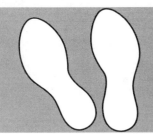

Lining Up

Color Line-Up

When calling children to line up, reinforce their color recognition skills in a variety of ways. This will also teach them to think and listen carefully. Here are some ideas:

- *Line up if you are wearing blue.* (a specific color)
- *Line up if you are wearing red socks.* (a piece of clothing of a specific color)
- *Line up if you are wearing g-r-e-e-n.* (spell the color word)
- *Line up if you have brown eyes.* (or hair)
- *Line up if your favorite color is red.*

You Choose

Play a game with attributes when lining up. When it is time to get in line, choose a child to go first. Start the game by saying her name and stating something that you have in common. For example, *Katie can line up because we both have a brother.* (Other attributes might be the same color clothing, same first letter of last name, both wearing glasses, both having hot lunch, both like to read Dr. Seuss books.) The first child then gets to pick the next one to line up. They say their name and an attribute they have in common. The game continues until everyone is in line.

Rhyme Time

When children are quiet and ready to be called to line up, go around the room and say a word from a common word family to each student. When a student tells you a rhyming word, they may get in line.

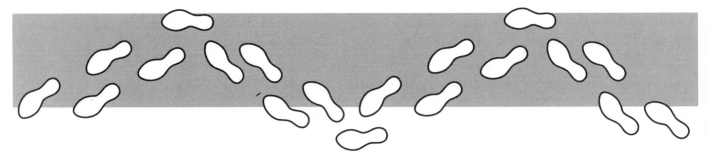

   0-7682-2607-4 *Great Rooms! Grades K–1*

Lining Up

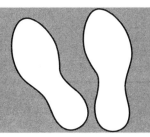

Math Line-Up

Sharpen your students' listening and math skills by calling them to line up according to math-related criteria such as the following:

- *If you have an even number of people in your family.*
- *If you are the oldest child in your family.*
- *If you can name or show me a triangle in the room.*
- *If you have three buttons.*
- *If you can tell me how many cents are in a nickel.*
- *If your birthday is in a summer month.*
- *If you can tell me what number comes after 14.*

Helping Hands

Having an established procedure for children to use in requesting help saves instructional time. Teach your students to use the *Helping Hands* on page 82. When they need help from you, they can stand it up on their desk or computer. Copy the hands on heavy red paper or have the children color them red so they are easy for you to spot. Have the students cut out a hand, fold it along the two dotted lines to form a base, and tape it together. The hand should stand up on its own. If the hand is tippy, attach a large paper clip to the base to weight it.

Be Right Back!

Copy the *Be Right Back!* signs on page 83 and give one to each student. Have the children write their name on it, color the picture, fold along the dotted lines, and tape the ends together to make it a three-sided stand-up sign. Teach the children that if they must leave their work for a few minutes to speak to you or use the restroom, they can put their Be Right Back sign at their place to save it. The sign will indicate to other students that the item (book, puzzle, computer, center project) is in use. Teach the children to honor the signs by not touching the work left behind.

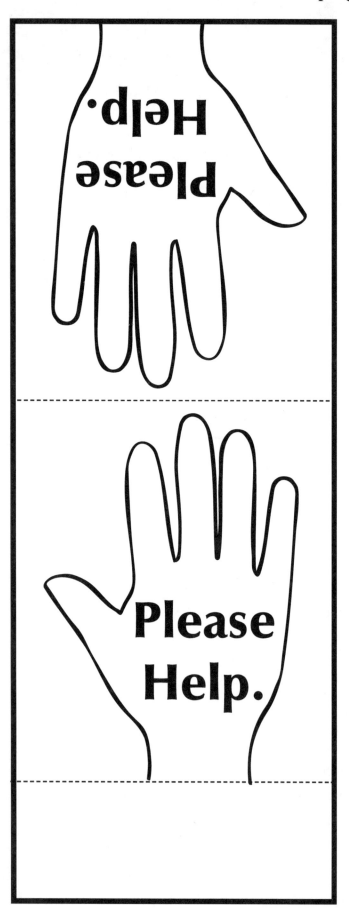

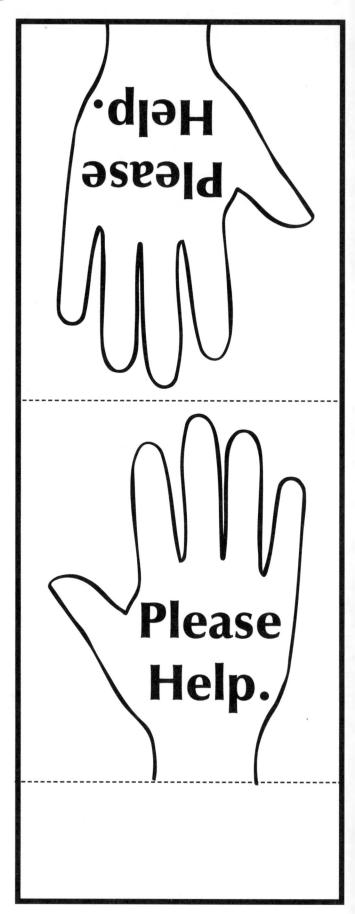

0-7682-2607-4 *Great Rooms! Grades K–1*

Be Right Back

0-7682-2607-4 *Great Rooms! Grades K–1*

Classroom Helpers

Classroom Helper Stars

Determine which jobs you will need and how often you wish to change helpers before introducing them to the children. Rotating jobs once a week should allow each child an opportunity to do each job. New jobs can be added as needed. Introduce each job and teach the way it should be carried out. You can select the person for each job randomly and keep track of the jobs each child has had on a class list. The children will probably be able to tell you if they have already had a job assignment, as well. Use the stars and signs on pages 85–87 to make a *Classroom Helpers* bulletin board display. Make multiple copies of the stars so you can write each child's name on one. Have an aide or parent volunteer color, laminate, and cut them out along with the signs. Staple the signs onto the bulletin board and leave space to pin the children's stars next to their assignments.

Ending the Day Quietly

Bring the school day to a quiet close by slowing down the children's activity. Allow fifteen minutes at the end of the day for the children to write in a journal or read quietly while you play some classical music. This will give you a few minutes to organize notes and papers to go home or to confer with individual children. It will give the children a peaceful start home.

Where Do I Go?

Once your class has an established routine at dismissal, make a chart that tells who rides the bus, who walks or is picked up by a family member, who goes to childcare, and who stays for on-site after-school care. Keep the chart in an accessible place and be sure to write a note in your substitute folder to tell your substitute teacher where to find it.

Talk About the Day

Spend ten minutes at the end of the school day talking about the day's activities. Have the children tell you what they enjoyed doing and make notes on the board. What was the best part of the day? What was the worst? List the activities they can relate when parents ask, *What did you do in school today?* Have each child tell you one thing from the list when it is time to line up.

Classroom Helper Stars

0-7682-2607-4 *Great Rooms! Grades K–1*

Messenger

Librarian

Mail Person

Teacher's Assistant

Materials Manager

Pledge Leader

Paper Manager

Song Leader

0-7682-2607-4 *Great Rooms!* Grades K–1

Classroom Helper Signs

Line Leader
Plant Care
Door and Light Person
Pencil Sharpener
Secretary
Pet Care

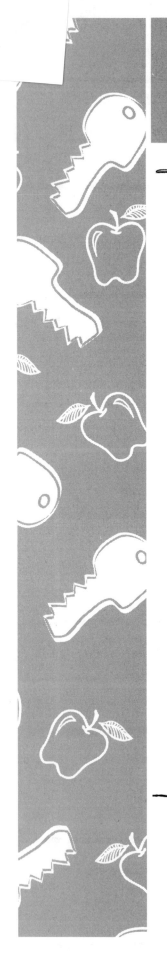

Substitute Teacher

Add a bingo or lotto game

Though you do not plan to be sick, it is wise to make a substitute plan at the very beginning of the year. No one wants to be sick and writing sub plans at the same time! Label a brightly colored pocket folder with "Substitute Folder" and your name, grade, room number, and school. Make copies of the forms on pages 89–92, complete the information, and place them in the folder. Also include information and items from the following list:

- Welcome note
- Lesson plans or substitute plans
- Class list
- Group lists for small group instruction

- Seating chart
- Dismissal chart for transportation
- School map
- Emergency procedures

Alternative Plan

If you are planning to be out of the classroom for a one-day conference or seminar, you may find it useful to make an alternate lesson plan for a substitute instead of having her follow your lesson plan book. As always, it is a good policy to over-plan. Have some extra work available in case it is needed. Make enough copies of reproducible word puzzles or math games for the class and have them on hand. Including a simple and fun-to-do art project in your plans is a good idea. Make it a project that both teacher and children will enjoy creating. You might also include a commercial lotto game that reinforces phonics or math skills. Planning activities that you know your students enjoy and excel at can make the day brighter for everyone.

Substitute File

Keep a set of plans and materials in a special file so they are ready for use whenever needed with a minimum of last-minute preparation on your part. Having a special file of substitute activities that you can pull at a moment's notice makes the job of planning for a substitute easier. Clip and save quick-and-easy ideas from teachers' magazines that can augment your lessons. Glue them on index cards and keep them in a file box. It will be simple to select and paper clip them to your plans.

0-7682-2607-4 *Great Rooms! Grades K–1*

Substitute Teacher Information

Thank you for serving as a substitute in our classroom. This form contains information that should help you throughout the day.

Today, you are substituting for _____ Grade _____

School Personnel	Location
Principal	_____
School Secretary	_____
School Nurse	_____
Librarian	_____
Classroom Aide	_____
Other K–1 Teachers	_____
Custodian	_____

If you need assistance, please contact _____ in room _____.

Students Who Can Help:

_____

_____

_____

These are Students with Special Needs:

Name	Comment
_____	_____
_____	_____
_____	_____

© McGraw-Hill Children's Publishing 0-7682-2607-4 *Great Rooms! Grades K–1*

Substitute Teacher Information

You can find these items in the following locations:

Lesson plans _____

Teacher manuals _____

Student emergency cards _____

Nearest restroom _____

Teacher's lounge _____

These students leave the classroom to work with a specialist:

Name	Days	Time	Room	Teacher

Schedule	Time	Special Duty	Day	Time
Class Begins				
Recess				
Lunch				
Recess				
Dismissal				
Other				

Classroom Procedures

These are our usual routines/procedures:

Opening _____

Attendance _____

Lunch Count _____

Restroom Use _____

Water Fountain _____

Recess _____

Library _____

Free Time _____

Discipline Techniques: _____

_____

Rewards _____

Consequences _____

Dismissal _____

Emergency or Drills: _____

_____

_____

_____

These students have a medical condition:

_____

_____

_____

Class Evaluation Form

Dear Substitute,

Thank you for teaching today. I hope your day goes well. Please take a few minutes after school to complete this form.

Sincerely,

_____

Overall, the class behavior was...

Excellent   Good   Fair   Poor

The following students were exceptionally helpful throughout the day: _____

_____

Were there any behavior problems during the day?   Yes   No

If Yes, please explain:

Were there any problems with lessons today?   Yes   No

If Yes, please explain: _____

_____

_____

Additional comments: _____

_____

_____

_____

_____
Substitute's name

0-7682-2607-4 *Great Rooms! Grades K–1*

Chapter 4: Paperwork

Read this chapter to find out about:

- handling student work
- collecting student work
- storing student work
- grading papers
- homework
- communication
- files
- report cards

Number, Please

Handling student papers is made more efficient by using a numerical system. Alphabetize the children's names and then number the list. Teach your students to write their name and assigned numbers on every paper. It is then a simple matter to organize the papers by number in order to record completed assignments or to file work samples. A student helper can easily put the papers into numerical order for you, saving valuable time. When new students are added to your class list, there is no need to shuffle numbers, just use additional ones.

© McGraw-Hill Children's Publishing

0-7682-2607-4 *Great Rooms! Grades K–1*

Student Work

Computer List

Keep a numbered class list on a computer word-processing system, so you can make additions. Print out multiple copies of the numbered list and clip them together. Leave space at the top or bottom of the list to write in a title. In this way you will always have a list on hand to check off things you want to keep track of. The lists are useful for recording who has brought in their supplies or permission slip, who has had a turn to work on the science mural or finished their Mother's Day gift, who has counted from 1 to 100, and so on. Enlarging the names on the list makes it easy to print off labels or tags for future use.

Desktop Nametags

To help children remember their assigned numbers, write each child's name along with his number on a nametag attached to his desk. Desk nametags not only serve as a handwriting model, but as a reminder to write one's name and number on all work. See page 95 for nametags that can be copied onto heavy paper for this purpose. Laminate the nametags to make them durable.

Finished Work

Designate a plastic tub or cover a small box with colorful adhesive paper and add the *Finished Work* label. (See page 96.) Teach the children to place their papers in the box facing up, with name and number in the top right corner. To help them remember, copy and cut out the cute animal character from page 96. Mount this picture in the Finished Work box as a reminder of how to place papers correctly. Tell students they may say hello to the animal when they put their work in the box, but only if they have remembered to write their name and number at the top of their papers.

0-7682-2607-4 *Great Rooms! Grades K–1*

Desktop Nametags

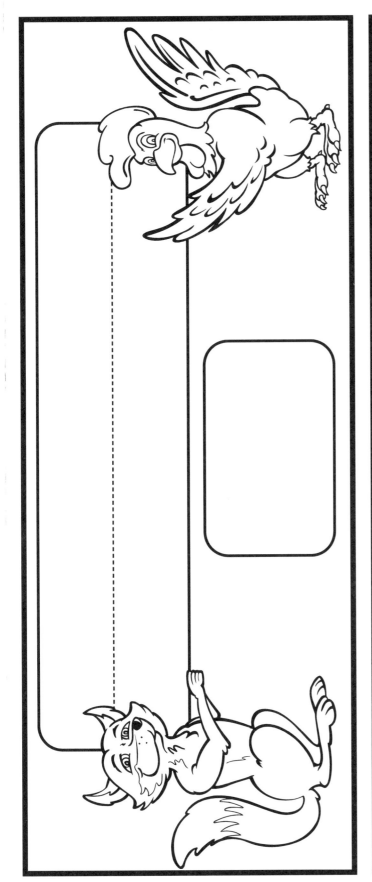
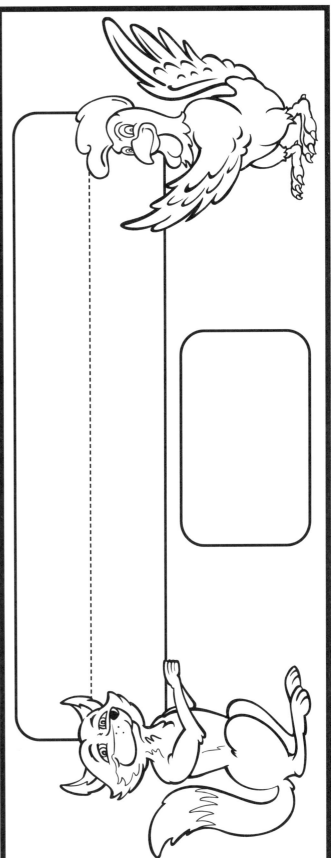

95

0-7682-2607-4 *Great Rooms! Grades K–1*

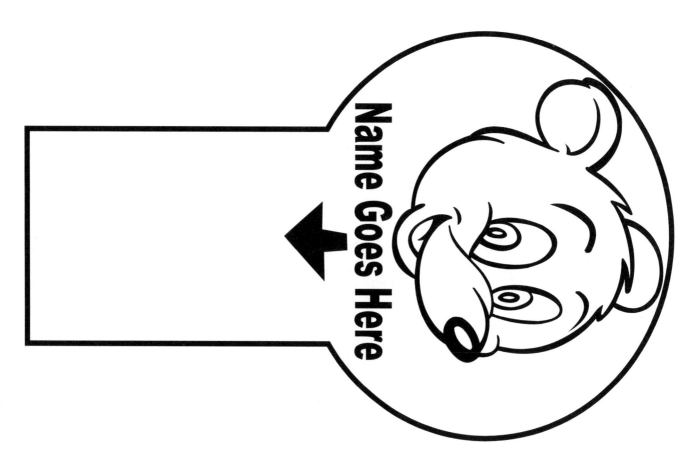

0-7682-2607-4 *Great Rooms! Grades K–1*

Handling and Storing Student Work

Names on Papers

When finishing a group assignment, have the children point to their names on their papers. This engages them in taking action and saves you from having to repeat the direction "Write your name on your paper" again and again.

Work Folders

Label file folders with your students' names and numbers. Have them place their work in the folders. Teach students to take out one assignment at a time, complete it, and replace it in the folder. When all papers are completed, they can place their work folder standing up in an open file box.

My Best Work

Allow students to select one paper each week to place on a bulletin board display of *Our Best Work*. Use bulletin board trim or strips of construction paper to divide the board into a grid with a space for each child's name. Make the children responsible for selecting work to put on the board. When papers are removed, have them file their papers in "My Best Work" folders. Save the folders to share with parents at conference time.

Student Portfolios

Collect student work that will help you assess children's development and skill mastery. Place these papers in individual student portfolios. Legal size file folders may be used for this purpose. Use these at report card and conference time to substantiate your evaluations. Be sure that all papers are dated so work can be seen in proper perspective.

Portfolios-to-Go

Once a month or every two months, send home a portfolio of work selected by the students. Write a letter asking parents to review the work, to write a comment at the bottom of the letter, and to return it to school with the portfolio (if you wish to make the portfolio cumulative). Make in-school portfolios from two large pieces of white drawing paper taped along three edges to form an envelope. Save these envelopes for the classroom and have students make their own "Portfolios-to-Go" to transport their work. Have students decorate drawing paper or construction paper and write their names on one side. Staple three sides. Place the work inside and fold over and staple the fourth edge so papers will stay securely inside on the trip home.

Handling and Storing Student Work

Alternative Ways to Correct Papers

There are many ways to accomplish the job of correcting student work. Put some of these ideas to work for you in order to save valuable instructional time. Once papers are checked, a quick scan will tell you who understood and who needs more instruction.

Partner Exchange—Direct partners to exchange papers, correct each other's work, and sign their name at the bottom.

Correcting Station—Let students show you their practice papers are complete and then go to a table that has an answer key and red pencils to check their work.

Self-Check—Have students color over their math answers with a yellow crayon. They can check their own work as you read the answers. (The yellow crayon prevents erasing answers.)

Teacher Highlights—Instead of correcting all student writing, use a highlighter to mark the best sentence, word, or letter written on the page.

How to Reduce Paperwork

Give children the practice they need without creating piles of paperwork.

- During group work, ask questions and have students use individual wipe-off boards to write their answers. For example, *Who can change the* m *in map to make a new word?*

- Teach the children to use hand signals to answer yes or no in response to your questions. Have them raise their hands and show one finger for yes and two for no, or thumbs up for yes and down for no.

- Have children hold up number or letter cards to answer questions you ask. For example, *What letter sound do you hear at the end of bus?*

- Use computers and interactive software programs in place of worksheets to give children reinforcement and practice in phonics skills or math facts.

We Are All Unique

By planning lessons that address different learning styles and involve multiple intelligences, teachers can reach students through their strengths. This can also reduce the amount of paperwork in the classroom. To replace paper-and-pencil activities, consider painting, creating with clay, dancing, drama, exploring how things work, making music, using the outdoors, working cooperatively, working with a partner, and quietly reflecting on what has been learned.

Homework

Read with Me

School district homework guidelines vary and you will want to find out what is expected at your grade level. Although homework assignments are often optional at the kindergarten level, you may choose to have a program of ten or fifteen minutes of daily reading time. Ask parents to share books, talk about books, and listen to their child read (tell the story, point to pictures, and so on). This exposure to books and reading is invaluable to a child's language development. To keep track of daily reading time, provide a folder for each child with a book and a form inside for parents to record time spent reading together. (See page 100.) Have the children take home their folders every Monday and return them on Friday. Keep track on a chart of the cumulative hours spent reading at home by your class. Have a Reading Celebration when 500 hours (or another appropriate number) are reached.

Homework Folders

Keep first grade homework organized and teach children responsibility for their work by using a folder system for homework, whether it is one day a week or daily. Use a sturdy pocket folder for each child and label it with the child's name and room number. Daily assignments or unfinished work to be completed at home can go in one pocket. The other pocket can hold longer-term or standing assignments such as daily spelling word practice and a reading log. Use your computer to type out instructions for standing assignments and staple these onto a pocket. Instructions might include a spelling activity for each day of the week, a list of weekly book report activities to choose from, and so on. You might also include a weekly check-off assignment sheet. (See page 101.) Help the children to write down their assignments each day. Ask parents to sign every day as assignments are completed. On Friday, collect the assignment sheets and have the children prepare their folders for the following week.

_____ Date_____

Daily Reading

Day

Minutes

Parent Signature

Day	Minutes	Parent Signature
Monday		
Tuesday		
Wednesday		
Thursday		
Friday		

Total
Minutes

© McGraw-Hill Children's Publishing

0-7682-2607-4 *Great Rooms! Grades K–1*

Name_____ Date_____

Homework

Day	Assignments	Parent Signature
Monday		
Tuesday		
Wednesday		
Thursday		
Friday		

0-7682-2607-4 *Great Rooms! Grades K–1*

Returning Student Work

Taking It Home

A folder for completed work can be used to help ensure that all the children's work will get home. Label a pocket-type manila file folder with each child's name and have her decorate it. Or for a more durable work folder, make a file pocket by having the children decorate legal-size file folders. Open the folders and laminate them. Then close them and staple the sides to form a pocket. Tape the side edges with colorful plastic tape to cover the staples. The children can take home their folders with completed work inside to show parents and bring the folders back empty the next day.

Postcards from the Ledge

Prepare postcards at the beginning of the year by addressing them to each child's parents. Commercial postcards are available through teachers' supply stores and catalogs. Or purchase postage-paid postcards from your post office. Use these postcards throughout the year to jot a positive note to parents regarding their student's successes. Addressing them ahead of time will help you ensure that each child receives postcard praise sometime during the school year. If you plan on mailing more than one item throughout the year, you may want to create address labels on your computer to save time.

Parent Post

Designate a bulletin board area near the door of your classroom for posting school notices and copies of letters that go home each week. Parents can check to see if any important notices, school calendars, or lunch menus did not make it home. Send a friendly e-mail note to those parents who have computers and have given you their e-mail address.

Quick Notes

Quick notes help you communicate with parents about children's successes and needs. Make multiple copies of the *Quick Notes* on page 103 to keep on hand. Send one home when a child achieves learning milestones, such as writing her name, counting to 100, skipping, hopping on one foot, or identifying all the letters of the alphabet. Parents will appreciate sharing their child's achievements. You can also use the notes to request that parents teach their children such things as zipping up a jacket, tying shoes, putting on boots, or learning their phone number or address.

0-7682-2607-4 *Great Rooms! Grades K–1*

0-7682-2607-4 *Great Rooms! Grades K–1*

Communication

Kindergarten News

Sending home newsletters to parents does not have to be a time consuming task. Simply use the form on page 105 to jot down a sentence or two of information each day, or use a software program to make a similar template on your computer. The children can help you compose the sentences on the board at the end of the day. This is a good way to refresh their memory of what they did in school each day. You can write the sentences onto a copy of the newsletter form. At the end of the week, add any special reminders, events, or positive comments in the extra block provided. Copy and send home the newsletter on Friday. Children will likely remember some of the things they wrote for the newsletter during the week and can talk about them with their parents.

First Grade News

Just a few minutes a day are all that is needed for you to keep parents abreast of what is happening in each curriculum area in your first grade classroom. Use the block form on page 106 to create your newsletter, or make a similar template on your computer. Draw the same form on the board and leave it for the week. Take a few moments near the end of each school day to have the children help you jot a sentence in a newsletter block telling what they did in one or more subject areas. For example, *We are working on our rain forest stories. We learned a dime is worth ten cents*. At the end of the week it is a simple matter to copy the sentences onto a newsletter form and add any information you want to communicate about upcoming events or the class's achievements. Photocopy and send home the newsletter on Friday.

Stamp It

Have rubber stamps made with useful phrases to help you communicate to parents in regards to their children's papers. Stamps such as *Please Sign and Return, Please Complete at Home*, and *Completed with Teacher's Help* will keep parents informed and help you enlist their aid.

Kindergarten News

Date_____

Monday

Tuesday

Wednesday

Thursday

Friday

Notes:

0-7682-2607-4 *Great Rooms! Grades K–1*

First Grade News

Date_____

Reading/Writing/Spelling

Math

Science/Social Studies

Other

Special Events

0-7682-2607-4 *Great Rooms! Grades K–1*

Files

Creating Files

An easy policy to follow when creating curriculum files is to start a general file and then subdivide it when it becomes full, creating smaller files on more specific topics. For example, you might start a file folder for Reading Ideas and Activities. After a few months you may find that the file is getting full. Take five minutes to subdivide it into files for beginning sounds and blends, phonics games, comprehension strategies, and word wall activities. It is easiest to set a goal of subdividing just one file at a time, rather than making time to organize an entire file drawer. In this way, your files will stay organized as they grow and your materials will be at your fingertips.

Curriculum File Organization

Here are some things to consider keeping in a curriculum file to help you with future lesson planning:

- A list or copy of state and/or district standards for the subject area
- Lesson plans with notes on what worked and what needed improvement
- A list of materials for each lesson telling where they are stored (media center, top shelf of closet, cupboard above sink, etc.)
- Ideas that you have jotted down or that other teachers have shared
- Ideas clipped from teacher magazines
- Photos of projects or displays

Administrative Files

You will not be overwhelmed by administrative paperwork if you set up files for each type of school communication that reaches your desk. By making files for them, you will be able to easily access and refer to principal's newsletters, central administration memos, school calendars, staff meeting agendas, and letters you have sent home.

0-7682-2607-4 *Great Rooms! Grades K–1*

Files/Report Cards

Desktop File

Create a system of mailboxes to help you sort and file your school mail efficiently. Use commercial stacking trays or make mailboxes from cereal boxes. Cut off the tops of five boxes, stack them horizontally with the openings facing out, and staple them together. Reinforce with mailing or strapping tape, then cover with adhesive-backed paper. Label the boxes *In*, *Out*, *Action*, *File*, and *Read*. When you receive mail, place it in the In box until you can scan it sometime during the day. When you have two or three minutes, scan and sort your mail. If you need to pass something along to a staff member or parent, place it in the Out box with a stick-on note bearing the person's name. If you need to take action on something, such as write a meeting date on your calendar, order a pocket chart, or register for a class, place it in the Action box. If the piece of mail is a memo, newsletter, or catalog that should be filed for future reference, place it in the File box until you or an aide can file it. Finally, place magazines and new materials that will require more time to read in the Read box. With this system you will know where things are and be better able to handle priorities. Remember to use the "round file"—your wastebasket (or a recycling bin)—for junk mail.

Report Card Talk

Spend a few minutes with children on an individual basis to discuss their progress report. You can do this before or after holding parent conferences. Make a brief checklist of possible discussion points and check off only those that pertain to the student. Sign and send home the checklist so parents know what you have discussed and the goals you have set together.

Dear _____,

My teacher and I have talked about some ways I can do better in the areas that have a checkmark.

❏ Keep up the good work in _____.
❏ Be a good listener.
❏ Finish all work.
❏ Cooperate with others.
❏ Keep cubbyhole neat.
❏ Remember homework folder.
❏ Practice _____ at home.
❏ _____

_____   _____
Student's signature   Teacher's signature

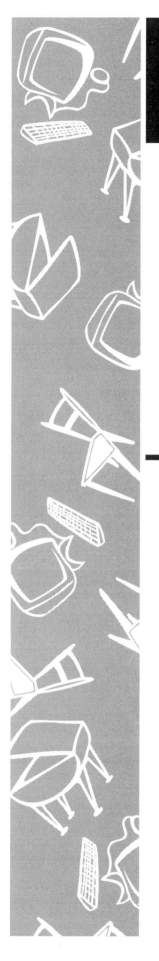

Chapter 5: Learning Centers

Read this chapter to find out about:

- arranging the classroom
- scheduling students
- keeping students accountable
- collecting work
- storing materials
- establishing rules
- assessment
- planning
- center ideas

Room Arrangement

Using cubbyholes, easels, and bookcases to create smaller spaces for centers is a good idea. A small space can hold fewer distractions for children who need help staying on task. Smaller spaces also help limit the number of children at a center at any one time.

However, be sure that you can view the children and thereby always supervise them.

Arranging the Classroom

Center Placement

When planning your classroom arrangement to accommodate learning centers, keep in mind different noise levels. Place centers with potentially higher noise levels, such as art, blocks, and construction centers, away from those that require quieter levels, such as reading, writing, and listening centers. Art centers, water and sand tables, and science centers are best placed in an area without carpeting so the floor can be easily cleaned after spills. They should also be near a sink, if possible. Carpet will absorb sounds and provide quiet in dramatic play, blocks, and library centers. In your planning, remember that a listening center will need to be located near an outlet and a science center needs to be located near a window to provide light for growing things.

Around the Room

One method for arranging smaller spaces that can be seen by the teacher is to place the centers around the outside of the room. This will leave an open area for gatherings in the middle of the room. Wide-open spaces sometimes invite children to run rather than walk from place to place, so you may have to adjust your arrangement accordingly.

Marking the Boundaries

If you are short on furniture to define center spaces, use a length of brightly-colored plastic tape on the floor or hang a chart, a sign, or fabric from the ceiling. The children will think this is a fun way to define space and will aid in color recognition if you associate specific centers with specific colors.

0-7682-2607-4 *Great Rooms! Grades K–1*

Scheduling Students

Center Picture Cards

If you wish to allow children to choose their center work, you will need a system to limit the number of children allowed at each center. One way to do this is to make picture cards depicting each center. If you plan to allow four students at a center, make four picture cards for that center. Make the picture cards with a symbol for each center, such as a book (reading center), a pencil (writing center), and a puzzle (manipulative center). Place the same symbol on a sign at the center to help your students easily identify it. You can use the *Learning Center Labels* symbols on pages 112–114 to make picture cards by coloring and gluing them onto poster board. Laminate the cards. At center time, hold all the cards facedown and have each child pick one to determine the first center he will go to. Set a timer for 10 to 20 minutes. When it rings, have the children tidy up their area, choose another card, and move to another center.

Cans and Clips

Limit the number of students in a center by placing a large can, such as a coffee can, at each center. Cover each can with a different color of adhesive-backed paper or spray paint the cans at home. Use permanent marker to color clip-on clothespins the same as the cans. Clip several clothespins to the edge of the can of the same color. Place a can at each center. The clothespins will indicate how many children you wish to allow at the center. Teach the children to take a clothespin from the can and wear it on their shirts while they are working at that center. When they leave, they should clip it back on the edge of the can.

Group Rotation

When you first introduce center work to your class, you may wish to structure center rotation so that you know the children have gone to each center or station. This will allow you to teach them how to move from center to center as well. Simply assign each child to a group with a color name. Start off each color at a different center, and tell the children in what order they should visit the centers. Set a timer to indicate when it is time to change.

Learning Center Labels

0-7682-2607-4 *Great Rooms! Grades K–1*

0-7682-2607-4 *Great Rooms! Grades K–1*

0-7682-2607-4 *Great Rooms! Grades K–1*

Keeping Students Accountable

It's Your Choice

Allowing students to choose a center to work at will foster responsibility and increase their confidence. Use the labels from pages 112–114 to make a chart of Center Choices on poster board. Draw a line down the middle of the poster board and then horizontal lines to clearly define a box for each center. Glue a center symbol in each box. Hang the Center Choices chart on a hanging chart stand. To indicate their choice of a center, have the children clip a clothespin with their name to the outside edge of the chart. Limit the number of clothespins to four at each center. Or if you wish, indicate the number of children allowed at each center by placing that number of decorative stickers along the edge. Demonstrate how to clip one clothespin on at each sticker.

Paper Plate Choices

Children can choose their centers with a system of paper plates. Glue center symbols (see pages 112–114) onto sturdy paper plates. Display the plates at the children's eye level on a bulletin board. Each child can use a clip-on clothespin with their name to indicate which center they will be working at.

My Center Work

Use a daily or weekly sheet to keep track of children's center activities. See page 116 for *My Center Work* forms. Create a master copy to update the names of each center on the books provided. Make a copy for each child, and have students color in the books to indicate where they have been. You may choose to photocopy the center work cards on bright cardstock and purchase one of the many shape stampers that are available. Children will bring their center card to you and you can punch the corresponding center. Your students will love knowing when each center is completed.

0-7682-2607-4 *Great Rooms! Grades K–1*

My Center Work

Week Of_____

My Center Work

Week Of_____

0-7682-2607-4 *Great Rooms! Grades K–1*

Keeping Students Accountable

Sign In, Please

Keep track of the children who have visited each center by placing a sign-in sheet with a pencil at each one. Teach them to sign in before doing anything else at the center and to place a checkmark after their name when leaving. This will give them two opportunities to remember to record their visit.

Record Sheet

A simple record sheet placed at each center can help your kindergarten or first grade students keep track of their center work. See page 118 for a sheet that can be personalized for your class by writing a student's name in each shape. Instruct the children to color in the shape that has their name.

Color Charts

Placing a simple chart each week at each center will help you and your students keep track of which ones they have visited. Use the chart on page 119 to make a master copy, listing your students' names. Indicate the name of the center and the date, then post it at the center. Have the children color in the box next to their name and in the matching day column when they work at a center. If desired, color code the day headings to help children color in the correct box—Monday red, Tuesday blue, and so on—and place the matching color crayon each day at the center. A glance at each center's chart will tell you who has not yet been there and who may need to be assigned there. After practicing this process, it will soon become second nature to your class.

Center Folders

A more sophisticated way to keep track of center work as children gain confidence is with a completed work folder. Attach a check-off sheet to a color-coded file folder at each center. When students have completed an assignment at the center, they check off their name on the list and place their work in the folder. A copy of your class list can be used for this purpose.

0-7682-2607-4 *Great Rooms! Grades K–1*

_____ Center

Date_____

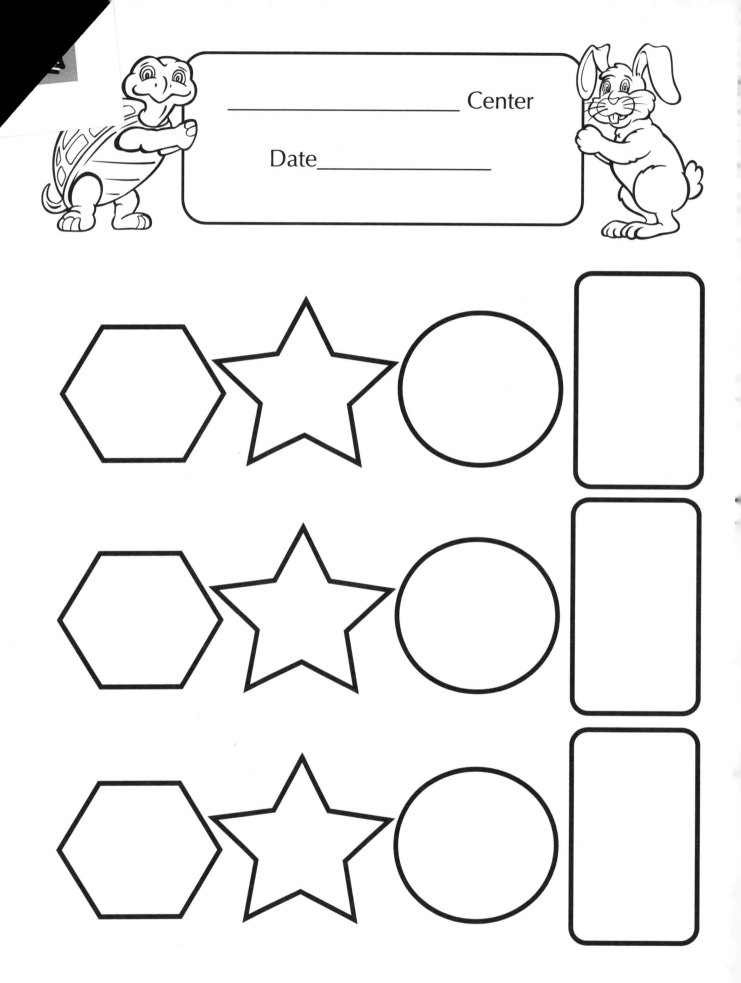

0-7682-2607-4 *Great Rooms! Grades K–1*

 Center

Student's Name	Mon.	Tues.	Wed.	Thurs.	Fri.
1.					
2.					
3.					
4.					
5.					
6.					
7.					
8.					
9.					
10.					
11.					
12.					
13.					
14.					
15.					
16.					
17.					
18.					
19.					
20.					
21.					
22.					
23.					
24.					
25.					
26.					
27.					
28.					
29.					
30.					
31.					
32.					

0-7682-2607-4 *Great Rooms! Grades K–1*

Where Does It Go?

Shoebox-size plastic boxes with lids can hold a variety of materials: math cubes, pine cones for science, old greeting cards for the art center, even small books in the library center. They can be easily stored on shelves where children can access them. When everything has its own place, children can learn to keep the center organized. Containers used in a center should be labeled front and back with a picture of what is inside and words describing the contents. The labels will give pre-readers a visual clue and enable beginning readers to acquire new reading vocabulary.

Color Coding 101

To make it easy for children to visually identify and store materials, make a storage tray from a soda can case or other shallow box. A large box lid can also be used. Cover it with adhesive-backed paper in a distinctive color or pattern. Cover smaller boxes that will fit inside the tray with the same paper. Teach the children that all the boxes of the same color or pattern are stored in that tray.

Color Coding 102

Store center materials in boxes of one color all on the same shelf. Mark each shelf by taping construction paper to the inside back of the shelf so children can see what color container belongs there.

Shadow Me

Cut out black paper shadows of the bottoms of containers of various sizes to show where they should be placed on a shelf. Use clear self-adhesive paper to protect them and keep them in place. Teach the children to place the containers on the shelf so the shadow is hidden. That is their clue that they have the right place.

Establishing Rules

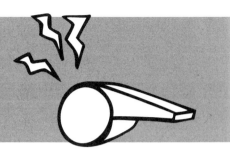

Working Rules

Establish working rules for the centers in your classroom so the children will understand what is expected of them. Teach them proper procedures and let them know what consequences follow improper behavior. If disruptions occur, give the children a reminder of what behavior is expected. Let the children know that if they engage in disruptive activity or activity unrelated to the center, they will be removed from the center. If things are not working on a particular day, it might be best to stop all center work. Gather the children to discuss the problem and work out solutions together.

Noise Meter

Consider using a reminder signal when noise levels get too high. Teach children a signal that they can give to each other as well. They can raise their hand in a peace sign (two fingers raised) to ask someone to please be quieter, or use the signal that has been predetermined for the entire class.

What to Do If I Get Stuck

Teach the children to consult with other students at a center first if they do not remember what to do in order to complete an activity. If they still need help, instruct them in what to do—raise hands, stand quietly by their tables, place a signal such as a stand-up sign at their work spaces, or place a craft stick with their name on it in your help jar.

Cleanup Time

Consider giving a two-minute warning before cleanup time. Teach the children a special signal reserved for this and instruct them in what they should do. For example, when the signal is given, they should finish what they are doing, file it, and check off the sign-in sheet. Signal cleanup time with a song. Emphasize participation from everyone. Since some centers require more cleanup, encourage the children to help each other until cleanup is complete.

Assessment

Looking for Growth

On-going assessment of your students' progress can be accomplished in several ways. One way is to collect the children's work in a portfolio and then compare current efforts with earlier ones. Conferencing with the children about their portfolios will help them learn to make their own self-assessments as well. Ask the children to tell you which paper is their favorite and why. Jot notes about your discussion, indicating areas done well and encouraging more of the same kind of work.

Observation

The teacher's observations during center time are a valuable assessment tool. You may wish to keep anecdotal records in a log (a spiral notebook or binder with paper) that has several pages for each child. Date your comments. If you find a logbook is too bulky to carry around with you, simply carry a packet of 3" x 3" stick-on notes. Use one to jot down the child's name and your observations. Then, place the notes on the child's pages in your logbook when time permits.

Focus on Literacy

Find ways to focus on literacy at every center. Giving children purposeful reading and writing activities to incorporate into their play helps them explore the world of literacy and come to understand the importance of reading. Provide multiple opportunities for your students to make and use lists, notes, messages, receipts, tickets, schedules, forms, memos, reminders, cards, menus, signs, labels, and tags. Make copies of the forms on page 123 and cut them apart. As you introduce each form at a center, explain how to fill it out and talk about how the form is used in the real world.

0-7682-2607-4 *Great Rooms! Grades K–1*

Ticket Shapes

LIST

1.

2.

3.

4.

5.

This belongs to:

ORDER PLEASE

TOTAL $

THANK YOU

TICKET TO

TICKET TO

NAME:

CARD NUMBER:

TOWN LIBRARY

This belongs to:

MESSAGES

0-7682-2607-4 *Great Rooms! Grades K–1*

Planning

Tell Me About It

Spend a few minutes each day after center work time to have the children share what they did, their accomplishments, and any problems they might have had during center time. This can be a time for you to observe what the children have learned and how individual children perceive their learning.

Planning Folders

A folder system makes planning center activities more efficient. It will take you less time to plan because ideas you have collected and student activity sheets will be in one place. Moreover, the system will allow you to reference props, materials, books, and activities used in previous years. Make a file folder for each center. Use folders in the same colors as the centers. Staple copies of the *Center Planning* forms from pages 125–126 in the front of each folder. Fill in the following information for each center: name of center, dates used (all year, November–December), and major skills and concepts addressed. Use the spaces to fill in materials used and the location where they are stored, as well as related books and where they can be found (classroom library, public library, borrowed from Mrs. C.). Indicate any special room set-ups if needed. On the second sheet, fill in the boxes with a brief description of each activity. At the bottom of the page, make notes on modifications you would make next time.

Meeting the Standards

To make sure that the center work you plan for your students brings them closer to achieving state or district standards, keep a list of the standards in your planning folder. Indicate on your planning sheet the number of the standard(s) being addressed by each activity. Circle the numbers to make it easy to spot which standards have received the most practice and which may need more.

0-7682-2607-4 *Great Rooms! Grades K–1*

Center Planning

Name of Center _____

Dates Used _____

Skills and Concepts

Materials / Location

Books / Location

Special Room Set-Up:

_____

_____

_____

Center Planning

Activity 1

Activity 2

Activity 3

Activity 4

Activity 5

Activity 6

Notes/Ideas/Review

0-7682-2607-4 *Great Rooms! Grades K–1*

Reading Center Ideas

The Reading Center is a place for children to explore books and other reading materials. They can read alone or with others in a comfortable atmosphere and discuss the ideas in books.

Reading Center Materials:

- Books previously read to the class
- Books on a theme the class is studying
- Books made by the class
- Chart stories
- Sentence strips in pocket charts
- *Pocket chart*
- Sentence building with word cards
- Familiar song lyrics and poems
- Book report forms
- Graphs of books read by the class

Reading Center Activities:

- Do choral reading with a partner.
- Take turns reading with a partner, reading every other page.
- Echo read with a partner. Repeat a sentence after your partner.
- Read to a stuffed animal.
- Read a book and fill out a book report.
- Use a copy of a chart story to put sentence strips in a pocket chart.
- Use a magic word wand to track the words to a poem on chart paper.
- Read a book. Write your name on a stick-on note. Put it on the page that has your favorite part.
- Read along with a book on tape.
- Read a book of classmates' names and pictures.
- Read a book and draw a picture about it.

All About Me
Class book of pictures + names
Vocab words of family members w/ pictures
My House book
Organize strips
Prem ~ Look in the Mirror Book ~ Who's in my family

0-7682-2607-4 Great Rooms! Grades K–1

Writing Center Ideas

The Writing Center is a place for children to write for a variety of purposes and to talk about their writing. They learn about print and the conventions of writing, such as spelling and punctuation. They also learn to write, revise, and publish their own works.

Writing Center Materials:

- Many sizes of writing paper
- Pencils, pens, markers, colored pencils, erasers
- Scissors, tape, and stapler for making books
- Colored paper for book covers
- Alphabet and alphabet cards
- Word resources, such as word walls and picture dictionaries
- Blank books

- Notebooks
- Word cards
- Individual journals
- Folders
- Wipe-off board, dry-erase markers, and an eraser
- Shallow box containing salt
- Writing visors
- Date stamp
- Stencils

Writing Center Activities:

- Draw a picture and label it.
- Write your name and classmates' names. Book of Names
- Use your finger to write letters or words in the salt box.
- Write a list of things you like to eat for lunch; shopping list
- Write a letter to a friend.
- Make a book about your family.
- Write in your journal about the question of the day. Stamp the date.
- Write a note to your teacher.
- Make a poster for a movie you saw; copy a book title and draw a picture
- Make a birthday card for someone.
- Make a dictionary of sight words

Kindergarten Centers

Blocks Center

At the Blocks Center, children experience a wide variety of lessons in science (gravity, balance), math (weight, size, shape), social skills (cooperation, caring for materials), verbal skills, motor skills, problem solving, and in using their imaginations.

Blocks Center Materials:

- Wooden blocks
- Blocks made from boxes filled with newspaper and taped securely closed
- Toy vehicles, people, and animals
- Area rug with roads on it
- Road signs
- Cardboard tubes

- Yardstick or measuring tape
- Blueprints
- Pictures of construction equipment and buildings
- Plastic toy tools
- Carpenter's aprons

Dramatic Play Center

Children develop social and communication skills at the Dramatic Play Center. They try on the roles of family members and workers they encounter in the community. The dramatic play center can change during the school year. It may start off as a home environment with kitchen appliances, table and chairs, and a baby bed. Later these props can be converted and added to in order to represent a store, an office, a restaurant, a hospital, and so on. The forms on page 123 can be used in the dramatic play center to encourage reading and writing activities. Store materials for each theme in a plastic storage box and label it. This will allow you to rotate the props in the center and coordinate them with your units of study. Here are some suggestions for props:

Grocery Store	cash register, play money, empty food containers, paper for signs, markers, shopping cart, aprons
Post Office	envelopes, stickers for postage, stationery, rubber stamp, address labels, junk mail, mailbox, pencils and pens
Restaurant	aprons, notepads for orders, pencils and pens, paper for writing menus and signs, calculator, cash register, burger baskets, pizza cardboard, fast food containers, plates, napkins, utensils, menus
Hospital	rolls of gauze, bandages, white shirts for lab coats, clipboard, toy doctor's bag with stethoscope, telephone, scale, poster board for signs, notepads for prescriptions, books about hospitals and doctors

0-7682-2607-4 *Great Rooms! Grades K–1*

Listening Center Ideas

In the listening center students develop their ability to learn aurally. They improve their listening vocabulary and practice skills involved in learning to read, such as phonemic awareness and phonics. They learn to follow verbal directions. They increase their awareness of music and musical instruments. Listening center materials, such as a book and tape or a tape and worksheet, can be stored together in plastic zipper-lock bags in a tub or hung on a pegboard.

Listening Center Activities:

- Listen to a tape of environmental sounds (car horn, dog barking) and identify them.

- Listen to songs from around the world sung in different languages.

- Listen to poems.

- Listen to a story and read along in the book.

- Make a recording of a favorite song.

- Listen to music and draw the colors you hear.

- Ask your partner a question and have him answer.

- Listen to your teacher's directions and complete a paper.

Art Center

The Art Center encourages children's creativity, decision-making, and self-expression. Here are a few helpful hints for the classroom Art Center:

- Limit the amount of materials children have to choose from at any one time.

- Rotate materials, such as chalk, tempera, watercolors, and markers.

- Introduce each material with instructions about how to use and care for it. For example, show how to rinse brushes and store them brush side up.

- Locate the center near a sink and on a washable surface. Use newspaper or a plastic tarp on the floor.

- Provide cleanup materials for the children (sponges, paper towels, wastebasket).

- Designate a table or shelf for wet or unfinished projects.

© McGraw-Hill Children's Publishing 0-7682-2607-4 *Great Rooms! Grades K–1*

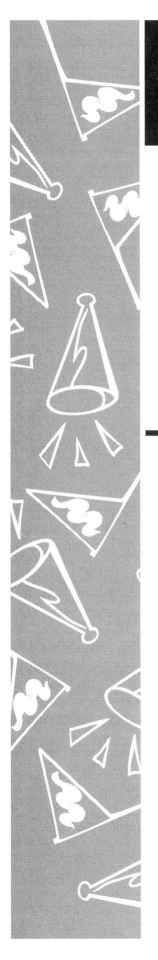

Chapter 6: Special Events

Read this chapter to find out about:

- first week of school
- Parent Night
- parent-teacher conferences
- field trips
- classroom visitors
- classroom celebrations
- testing
- end of the year

Bulletin Board Welcome

Prepare a special bulletin board for your students to complete on the first day of school. Title it "Kindergartners Up and Away" or "First Graders Reach High." Give each child a copy of page 133. Have students color their hot air balloon and draw themselves riding in it. Write kindergartners' names for them and post the pictures on the board. Assist first grade children in writing their own names and cutting out the balloons before you staple the artwork to the bulletin board.

0-7682-2607-4 *Great Rooms! Grades K–1*

First Week of School

Getting to Know You

Planning a get-to-know-you activity for each day of the first week of school will help children learn each other's names and start to build a sense of community in your classroom. Teach your class to sing this song to the tune of "Row, Row, Row Your Boat." Have children learn the name of the person with whom they shake hands.

Shake, shake, shake my hand.

Smile and say hello.

Will you be my friend today?

Smile and say hello.

—Barbara Allman

Learning to Read

Six-year-olds are often told they will learn to read in first grade. More than one child has gone home on the first day of school greatly disappointed because he did not learn to read! Children are usually able to read a number of environmental words when they start school. Point out to them all the words they are able to read with a grab bag activity on the first day of school. In a large bag, place food containers with labels that children are familiar with, such as cereal boxes or milk cartons. Also place in the bag pictures of traffic signs, such as STOP and SLOW, and ads cut from newspapers and magazines that have logos for grocery stores, fast food restaurants, gas stations, car dealerships, and so on. Have a child reach into the bag and hold up a container or picture for the class to see. If someone is able to "read" the words, list them on chart paper. When you are done, count the number of words on the list and congratulate the class on how many words they already know how to read! Invite the children to bring in other words from home to be added to the list.

Up and Away

0-7682-2607-4 *Great Rooms! Grades K–1*

Parent Night/Open House

School districts and schools have different ways of conducting parent nights in the fall. Whether your principal schedules a school-wide open house or you schedule your own one-hour meeting to establish a rapport with parents and orient them to the curriculum in your classroom, here are some hints to help make it a successful evening.

- Inform parents that you will not have time to discuss individual students at the open house, but that you will be happy to set up a time to talk about any specific concerns they may have about their children.

- Have your students decorate a Welcome banner with their names and pictures.

- Have the children write or decorate a reminder to take home the day of the open house.

- Display student work around the room. Parents will take pride seeing their child's work and will enjoy looking at the work of other children as well.

- Display your curriculum and samples of texts for reading, math, and other subjects.

- Prepare a clipboard with a sign-up sheet for parents who would like to volunteer.

- Play a tape recording of your students singing the songs they sing daily.

- Give a brief talk about goals for the year, the daily schedule, grading, homework policy, remedial and gifted programs, and classroom management system. Write the outline of your talk on the board. Make a summary handout as well for parents to take home.

- Play a videotape of children working at different centers.

- Allow time for parents to ask questions and to browse.

Drop a Note

Before parents leave on open house night, invite them to write a short note to their child and place it on the child's desk or mailbox. Set out colorful shape notepads and pens on a table for this purpose. Children will be delighted to find a special message waiting for them the next day. You may want to write a note to any children whose parents could not attend so that they do not feel left out.

Guest Register

Place an open guest register (notebook) and a pen on a table near the door of your classroom. At the open house, ask parents to sign it. This will help jog your memory later, and will allow you to mention to individual children that you spoke with their parents.

Parent-Teacher Conferences

Getting Ready for Parent Conferences

Once your conferences have been scheduled, use the schedule to sequence the students' portfolios by conference day and time. Also prepare a file folder for each child containing a copy of the progress report, work samples, test scores, reports from other school staff, a conference record form (see page 136), and a brief list of topics you wish to discuss. Write on the outside of the folder the conference day, date, and time. Organize these folders along with the portfolios and have them at another table near the conference table. In this way, the information you need for each conference will be immediately accessible.

Conference Reminders

Even though parents may have received an official notice from the school regarding their conference time, you may wish to send home a reminder the day before. Parents will appreciate a thoughtful reminder in advance. See page 137 for reminder notices.

Welcoming Atmosphere

Establish a welcoming atmosphere for parent conferences. Have the children help make the classroom look its best by cleaning their desks and cubbyholes. Display their recent work. If possible, use a table and chairs that are adult-sized for the conference. Situate these in an area of the room where conversations will not be overhead outside. A small vase of flowers or a plant on the table is a pleasant touch. Have on hand drinking water, paper cups, tissues, pens, and paper for notes. Setting a small clock on the table will remind you as well as parents that you are on a schedule.

Conducting a Conference

In a successful conference, both parents and teacher feel they have been heard and have established a partnership on behalf of the student. Here are some tips for conducting parent-teacher conferences:

- Greet parents at the door.
- Keep in mind that some parents may be uncomfortable in a school setting.
- Begin and end the conference with a positive comment about the child.
- Listen actively. Rephrase what is said to check your understanding.

- Take notes on important points discussed.
- Ask open-ended questions. Do not interrupt.
- Provide tangible information in the form of test scores, assessments, anecdotal records, and work samples.
- End on time.

0-7682-2607-4 *Great Rooms! Grades K–1*

Conference Record

Student Name _____

Conference With _____

Conference Date _____

Areas of Progress

Areas Needing Improvement

Goals: Suggestions

School:

Home:

Conference Reminder

Dear _____,

    I am looking forward to meeting with you about

_____ progress.

Date: _____

Time: _____

Room: _____

    Sincerely,

_____

Conference Reminder

Dear _____,

    I am looking forward to meeting with you about

_____ progress.

Date: _____

Time: _____

Room: _____

    Sincerely,

_____

0-7682-2607-4 *Great Rooms! Grades K–1*

Field Trips

Field Trip Guide

Field trips give your students a first-hand experience of their community and a break from everyday classroom routine. They are a wonderful opportunity to develop a curriculum theme and provide children with purposeful tasks in reading, writing, and many other subject areas. If possible, plan your field trips before the start of school as you study district curriculum guides and make long-range plans for the year. Your school or district may have a printed guide with information on suggested field trip destinations, fees, phone numbers, and contacts to help you.

Parent Helpers

To determine how many parent helpers you will need, talk to other teachers in your grade or your principal. More helpers will be needed the younger the children. You may want one parent for every two to four children. Prepare color-coded nametags (page 139), and have the parent helpers wear the same color as their group. Plan for more parent helpers than you need, so you will not be caught short if a child or parent is ill. Send home a letter to your volunteers on the day before the trip, outlining what you would like them to do. For example, make sure the children put on nametags and go to the bathroom before leaving school, check each student's supplies, and collect lunches. You might ask one parent to bring a cooler with ice to hold milk cartons. Have parents sit with their group on the bus. Let them know that they are responsible for seeing that the children in their group act appropriately. Ask the parents to arrive early and make sure you let them know how happy you are that they have volunteered their time. The children can write thank-you notes to the parent helpers upon their return, and you can add your thanks as well.

Ready-Set-Go

Here is a list of tips that can help you prepare your class for a field trip:

- Assign each student a partner. Be sure all children know who their parent helper is.
- Prepare an activity folder for each child with fun-to-do worksheets, such as puzzles, games, and booklets related to the theme of the trip. Children can do these on the bus or at breaks.
- Prepare a list of songs and poems your students will enjoy singing during the bus ride.
- Review classroom rules and remind the children that they apply on the bus, too.
- Label boxes for storing lunches. Show these to the children.
- Inform parents of the time the bus will leave. Explain that children who are late will stay with another teacher for the school day.

Field Trip Nametags

Name _____

_____

School_____

_____

Name _____

_____

School_____

_____

Name _____

_____

School_____

_____

Name _____

_____

School_____

_____

Name _____

_____

School_____

_____

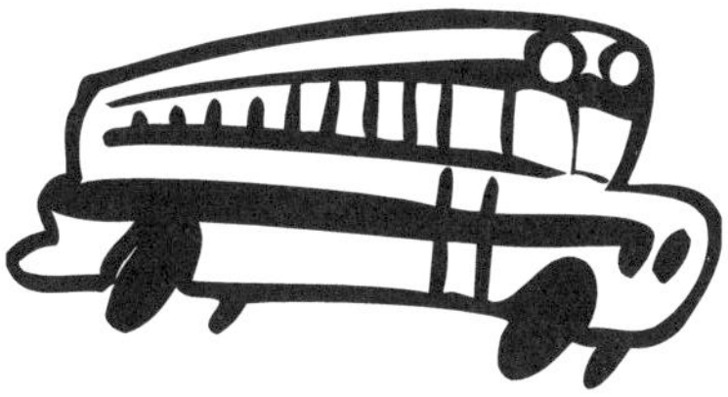

Name _____

_____

School_____

_____

0-7682-2607-4 *Great Rooms! Grades K–1*

Classroom Visitors

Inviting special speakers to your room brings the community into focus for the children in your class. These guest speaker events spark students' interest as they learn about different topics and the world around them. Parents are one of the best resources for special speakers. When you study the human body, invite a parent who is a healthcare professional to speak about the heart, medical equipment for people with handicaps, or another health topic. Perhaps a parent in the building trades can demonstrate tools and blueprints or bring heavy equipment to the school for children to see in action. Let parents know at your open house or with a letter what general topics you plan for the year that could be enhanced by a speaker.

Author Visits

Some school districts bring children's authors to their schools annually for an Author's Fair day. If your district does not have a program, you can contact authors through their publisher's Web site. Check with your school or town librarian for names of local authors. Here are some hints to make the most of an author's visit.

- Book the author well in advance (6 months to one year).

- Read the author's books aloud to your students before the visit. Make a classroom display.

- Research the author's background in *Something About the Author* (available in libraries) and share some of the information with the children.

- Help the children prepare meaningful questions. Write them on chart paper.

- If you plan a book-signing session, order books six to eight weeks ahead. Place on each book a stick-on note with the correct spelling of the owner's name, so the author can personalize her note.

- Have an older or more capable student act as ambassador if the author is visiting more than one classroom.

- Make a sign welcoming the author.

0-7682-2607-4 *Great Rooms! Grades K–1*

Classroom Celebrations

Happy Birthday

Have the children form a circle or "birthday cake" and have the birthday child stand in the center. Sing the Happy Birthday song. Have the birthday child put the right number of candles on their cake by choosing children to stand with them in the center.

As they take each candle by the hand, have the group count the candles one-by-one. At the end, the birthday child blows out the candles and they all fall down.

Birthday Treats

Choose a birthday treat from this list to become a tradition in your classroom.

- Eat lunch once a month with the children who have birthdays in that month.
- Make a giant birthday greeting signed by the class. (See page 14.)
- Have the birthday child choose a book for the teacher to read aloud.
- Have the birthday child be the teacher's assistant for the day.

New Siblings

Celebrating the birth of a new sibling gives the big sister or brother extra attention at a time when he or she may need some. Give the child a badge to wear that says "Big Brother" or "Big Sister." See page 142 for badges. Have the class tell about some of the funny things babies do and draw pictures of themselves when they were babies.

Losing a Tooth

When a child in your class loses a tooth, give them a special envelope in which to seal the tooth and carry it safely home. Make copies of the tooth on page 142 to have on hand. Help the child as needed to cut out, fold along the dotted lines, and glue or tape together the envelope.

0-7682-2607-4 *Great Rooms! Grades K–1*

Special Badges

0-7682-2607-4 *Great Rooms! Grades K–1*

Testing! End of the Year

Preparing for Tests

Most states and school districts administer standardized achievement tests at certain grade levels to assess student progress. If your school tests at your grade level, there are some things you can do to help children perform their best.

- Inform parents well in advance when testing will take place. Send home a reminder the day before the test. Ask parents to make sure their child gets enough rest.

- Ask parents to reassure their child and encourage a positive attitude.

- On testing days, arrange for students to have a nutritious breakfast at school and a nutritious snack.

- Familiarize your students with testing formats, such as filling in bubbles and marking the best answer of several choices.

- Give children opportunities to work alone.

Remember that a well-rounded curriculum will prepare your students for testing. Use the item analysis of last year's tests to help you pinpoint areas of the curriculum where you can enhance your teaching.

Ending the Year

Maintaining the same routine and procedures the last few weeks of school will help to keep your students on task and learning until the end of the year. Plan some activities to wrap up the year and help children look forward to moving to another grade.

- Prepare your kindergarten students for next year by taking a walk to the first grade classrooms. First grade students can write notes to the kindergartners telling them what fun things they will do.

- Make copies and distribute page 144 to create a Keepsake Autograph Book for each child. Adding blank sheets cut to fit will give extra room for classroom autographs.

- Save dismantling the room for the last part of the last day of school and have the students help. Hold a raffle for items you might otherwise toss that children may enjoy having.

0-7682-2607-4 Great Rooms! Grades K–1

Autograph Book

School Year

_____

My teacher's name was

_____

My Autograph Book

Name_____
Date_____
School_____
Grade_____

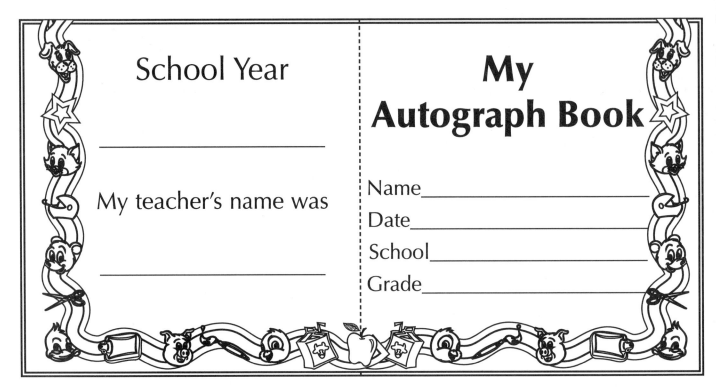

My friends at school

My friends at school

0-7682-2607-4 *Great Rooms! Grades K–1*